AMERICAN HORTICULTURAL SOCIETY
PRACTICAL GUIDES

HEDGES

AMERICAN HORTICULTURAL SOCIETY
PRACTICAL GUIDES

HEDGES

MICHAEL POLLOCK

A Dorling Kindersley Book

Dorling **DK** Kindersley

LONDON, NEW YORK, SYDNEY, DELHI, PARIS,
MUNICH and JOHANNESBURG

PROJECT EDITOR Simon Maughan
DESIGNER Janice English
SERIES EDITOR Annelise Evans
SERIES ART EDITOR Ursula Dawson
US EDITOR Mary Sutherland
MANAGING EDITOR Anna Kruger
MANAGING ART EDITOR Lee Griffiths
DTP DESIGNERS Louise Paddick, Louise Waller
PRODUCTION MANAGER Sarah Coltman

First American Edition, 2001
2 4 6 8 10 9 7 5 3 1
Published in the United States by
Dorling Kindersley Publishing, Inc., 95 Madison Avenue, New York, NY 10016

Dorling Kindersley Publishing, Inc. offers special discounts for bulk purchases for sales
promotions or premiums. Specific, large-quantity needs can be met with special editions,
including personalized covers, excerpts of existing guides, and corporate imprints.
For more information, contact Special Markets Department, Dorling Kindersley Publishing, Inc.,
95 Madison Avenue, New York, NY 10016 Fax: 800-600-9098

Library of Congress Cataloging-in-Publication Data

Pollock, Michael, 1938-
Hedges / Michael Pollock
      p. cm. -- (AHS practical guides)
   Includes index.
   ISBN 0-7894-7128-0 (alk. paper)
   I. Title.
   II. Series.

SB473 .P83 2001
635'.9'76--dc21   00-056043

Reproduced by Colourscan, Singapore
Printed and bound by Star Standard Industries PTE Ltd, Singapore

see our complete catalog at

www.dk.com

CONTENTS

USING HEDGES IN THE GARDEN 6

An introduction to hedges and the many reasons to
grow them in a garden; hedges for borders, screens,
or shelter; formal and informal hedges in garden design;
fruiting and flowering hedges; and hedges with attractive
leaves and stems.

LOOKING AFTER HEDGING PLANTS 34

RECOMMENDED HEDGES 54

An alphabetical guide to some of the most reliable plants
for both formal and informal hedging, including descriptions
of foliage, flowers, and fruits.

USING HEDGES IN THE GARDEN

WHAT IS A HEDGE?

THERE ARE ALL SORTS OF HEDGES found around us in the countryside and in gardens and yards. A hedge is most usually formed from a row of closely planted trees or shrubs kept attractive and contained in height and spread by regular cutting. Almost any woody plant can be grown as a hedge, but some are particularly suited to this type of growth. This book tells you how to grow hedges and their usefulness and interest as garden features.

DIFFERENT TYPES OF HEDGING

Most hedges are no more than 15ft (4.5m) in height – often shorter for ease of management – and taller plantings are better known as shelter belts, which are suitable for very large yards, estates, and farmland. Shrubby hedges kept less than 18in (45cm) in height are referred to as edging. These make interesting features along pathways or for making formal garden patterns. Once established, most hedges form screens, although not all screens are hedges.

The term "fedge" is sometimes used to describe wooden support structures that are combined with bamboos or with climbing plants, such as roses and clematis, to form a hedgelike screen or border. For a break from tradition, these are well worth thinking about in a garden plan.

FANCY FEDGE
A fence or trellis that is combined with climbing or nonclimbing plants is often known as a fedge: a cross between a fence and a hedge. Here, roses growing along a wooden support provide an attractive, informal garden feature.

◄ THREE TIERS *A formal yew hedge is fronted by a lavender hedge, then boxwood edging.*

WHY PLANT A HEDGE?

THE PRIMARY REASON FOR PLANTING A HEDGE is usually to mark out and maintain the boundaries of a property or a space within it, with the secondary objective to create a sense of privacy. Both these reasons are connected with the common instinct for establishing our own territory. Walls and fences meet these needs, but plants offer so much more in terms of beauty and other, less obvious benefits, such as wind protection and improved security.

THE HIDDEN BENEFITS

Appreciated too little by gardeners are the real benefits that hedges have in a garden, and wind protection is perhaps the most important. Unlike a wall or fence, a hedge filters and calms the wind rather than totally obstructing its flow (*see pp.18–19*), which leads to improved air circulation and the formation of a sheltered microclimate. From the home-owner's point of view, this means improved growing conditions as a result of warmer ground temperatures, and the increased wind protection gives a garden a greater overall feeling of seclusion.

Hedges can contain children and some pets within its limits, and those armed with spines or thorns contribute to a home's security, since they can deter unwanted visitors. Perimeter hedges also have their uses when unwanted views, unattractive structures, or neighboring buildings need to be obscured. Conversely, such hedges can be cleverly placed so they frame a feature beyond and enhance the view from your yard or garden.

MORE THAN A BACKDROP
This dark English yew hedge makes a fine background to the summer border at its base. It also offers vital shelter.

A SECLUDED
MICROCLIMATE
*A garden or yard
enclosed within the
boundary of a hedge
can have a more
sheltered environment
than on the other side
of the hedge.*

OPPORTUNITY FOR DESIGN

Whatever the reason for growing a hedge, remember that it will be a prominent feature, and where planting anew provides a perfect moment to create something special in the garden's design. Hedges inspire ingenuity; to a gardener, they

---

Dark hedges make impressive backdrops to bright flower borders

---

offer the perfect opportunity to create illusions, to focus the eye's attention on particular details, or to make secluded spots for shelter or shade.

The first point of concern with any new hedge must be the practical aspect of establishment and eventual maintenance (*see pp.10–11*), but this is also the time for creative thinking. It is a chance to be imaginative and inventive with the plants at your disposal and the yard or garden space within which you need to work.

It is unfortunate that hedges are seen all too often as an uninspiring and purely functional garden feature, because they can provide many exciting possibilities for introducing color. Dark hedges, such as English yew and Lawson cypress, make impressive backdrops to flower borders, and they are sometimes used as living screens to separate beds or areas that are planted with contrasting colors and designs. Thoughtfully select species with attractive flowers, foliage, and fruits so the display provides interest all year. As a result, you may soon discover birds nesting in the shelter of your hedge and summer bees and butterflies feeding on nectar-rich flowers such as those of *Escallonia*, *Ceanothus*, common broom, firethorn, and lavender. If you enjoy nature, this will greatly extend your enjoyment of the garden.

A hedge strikes the perfect balance between our ornamental and territorial needs. It forms a gentle medium between the inflexible architecture of our homes and the unpredictability of nature.

PRACTICAL CONSIDERATIONS

THINK CAREFULLY BEFORE PLANTING A HEDGE, and give time to consider all the practicalities. In this way, expensive mistakes (such as wrongly matching a plant to the site) are avoided, and the final hedge is both useful and attractive. There are choices to be made according to purpose, cost, and climate, and to what you actually enjoy in a garden. A mix of hedging plants, for example, can be much more pleasing than a wall of a single evergreen species.

HOW MUCH WILL A HEDGE COST?

Wherever a long section of hedging is to be planted, cost will almost always be of relevance. Savings can be made if less expensive plants, which are often raised from cuttings or seeds (*see pp.50–51*), are used in less conspicuous parts of the garden, or if lengths of choicer, more expensive plants are kept short and used for areas of prime importance only. If one type of hedge plant is too expensive, there are usually several alternatives to choose from.

MAINTAINING A HEDGE

Plants that are naturally vigorous or allowed to grow tall will certainly be expensive and difficult to trim and maintain; in addition, they may simply demand too much of your time and physical capabilities. Therefore, it is essential to think many years ahead; always choose carefully a manageable hedge plant that will eventually fit within the scale of your yard or garden. Ask yourself this

> Tall hedges are notorious
> subjects of disputes
> between neighbors

question: several years from now, when both the hedge and I are older, will I still have the same energy for garden and hedge maintenance as I do now? The vigor and final height and spread of many different hedge plants can be found in the plant catalog, which begins on page 55.

LOOK BEFORE
YOU LEAP
It is essential to check before purchase and installation that plants are well matched to their site. For instance, not all plants will tolerate cold, snowy winters as well as this boxwood hedge.

◀ EASY TO KEEP
*Informal hedges,
such as this forsythia
(F. 'Lynwood'), are
relatively easy to
maintain.*

▼ COSTLY UPKEEP
*This beautifully
kept Leyland
cypress hedge is
very vigorous; only
by very frequent
trimming can it be
made to look like this.*

Dealing with an overgrown hedge is
unappealing, potentially hazardous, and
always hard work. Hedges that are allowed
to grow unchecked may eventually interfere
with overhead utility lines or encroach on
a useful garden area. Tall and unkempt
hedges may cast deep shade and obstruct
pleasant views – both notorious grounds
for disputes between neighbors. Hedges
should be contained for these reasons.

It is unwise to plant any woody hedge
plant in a position where its roots can
penetrate the foundations of buildings.
Similarly, be careful where you plant
moisture-loving hedge plants, such as
willows or alders. Sited close to drains,
their roots will seek them out as a source
of water and create obstructions.

RELIABLE HEDGE PLANTS

Berberis julianae Dense growth with strongly
spined leaves; yellow flowers in late spring.
Buxus sempervirens (Boxwood) Bushy, dark
green growth; can live for decades or more.
Cornus stolonifera (Red osier dogwood)
Deciduous shrub; dark red winter shoots.
Crataegus laevigata (English hawthorn)
Thorny branches; white flowers in spring.
Ilex crenata (Japanese holly) Small-leaved
holly; excellent boxwood substitute.

Juniperus chinensis Strongly scented, dark
green foliage; blue-black berries.
Lavandula angustifolia (English lavender) Gray-
green, aromatic leaves; purple summer flowers.
Rosa rugosa Dense, very prickly growth;
clove-scented flowers followed by red hips.
Sarcococca hookeriana (Sweet box) Compact
growth; very fragrant white flowers in winter.
Taxus baccata (English yew) Slow-growing,
dark green leaves; female plants bear red fruits.

SUITING THE SOIL

FUNDAMENTAL TO THE SUCCESS of a hedge is the selection of species that are most likely to thrive in your particular location. For example, alkali-hating plants will grow satisfactorily only in neutral or acid soils. A great deal can be learned by looking around your area to see what plants do well in the soil of local gardens; then, you can build on such observations with advice from nearby nurseries. Time put to prospecting possible pitfalls is time well spent.

SOILS AND LIME

The lime content of a soil directly influences the establishment and growth of plants. Since soils vary in natural lime content, and the needs of different plants vary, the particular tolerance of individual plant species to alkaline soil must be a special consideration when planning any hedge. Those sites markedly deficient in lime, which are described as acid soils, induce poor growth in many species; this is not only by reason of low calcium availability but because the uptake of other essential nutrients is interfered with.

Soils of high lime content are known as alkaline or chalky soils, and they too are unsuitable for some plants. Whereas it is quite possible to overcome soil acidity by applying ground limestone when preparing the hedge site (*see p.37*), reducing alkalinity in soils is a far greater challenge, and it cannot be recommended here.

> ### Always check the lime content of the soil before planting a hedge

A potential hedge site should always be checked for the natural level of soil acidity or alkalinity with a simple measuring device, in the form of a pH testing kit. They are available from most gardening suppliers.

PRETTY USEFUL
Mountain laurel (Kalmia latifolia) *is a versatile shrub that can be used in many difficult garden sites: it grows well in acid to neutral soils, it tolerates moisture-retentive ground, and it is happiest in partial shade. It bears clusters of pale to deep pink flowers from late spring to midsummer.*

◀ TOLERANT OF ACID SOILS
Black elder can grow into a tall hedge and is tolerant of acid soils. The large, creamy white heads of musk-scented, early summer flowers are followed by shiny black fruits later in the season.

▼ ALKALINE SOILS
Most weigelas tolerate alkaline soils. Shown here is W. 'Florida Variegata' – a cultivar with variegated leaves. It bears clusters of dark pink, funnel-shaped flowers during late spring and early summer.

SOILS AND WATER

Although some plant species, such as willows, poplars, and alders, thrive in wet places, the great majority fail if their roots become waterlogged and deprived of air. It is very important, therefore, to assess any potential hedge site for its drainage capacity. Are there hollows where water collects? Does a hole dug to two spade blades' depth provide evidence of any impenetrable layers, or retain water for a long period after rain? The drainage capacity of a valued site can often be improved by cultivation (*see p.37*) or by the laying of an artificial drainage system.

HEDGES FOR ACID AND ALKALINE SOILS

ALKALINE OR CHALKY SOILS
Deutzia Deciduous; white to pink flowers.
Escallonia Evergreen; white to red flowers.
Forsythia Deciduous; early yellow flowers.
Osmanthus Evergreen; white flowers.
Philadelphus (Mock orange) Deciduous; white flowers, often fragrant.
Prunus (Cherry) Deciduous or evergreen; white to red flowers.

ACID SOILS
Elaeagnus (Oleaster) Mostly evergreen; attractive foliage.
Ilex (Holly) Evergreen; glossy foliage and fruits.
Juniperus (Juniper) Evergreen; scented foliage.
Salix (Willow) Deciduous; attractive stems.
Sorbus Deciduous; tree forms with white flowers.
Tamarix Deciduous; pink flowers.
Taxus (Yew) Evergreen; attractive foliage.

Hedges for Borders

A WELL-MAINTAINED BOUNDARY HEDGE that consists of attractive plant species will add much to the character of a property, besides saying something about the gardener who lives there. It is an excellent way to mark the limits of an area, although in most cases the spread of a shrubby hedge will naturally encroach on land to either side of the actual perimeter line. This is a significant point to bear in mind where dispute over land ownership might arise or where there is a chance of gradual invasion of pathways.

Protective Borders

All hedges deter entry to an area, and they are also a way of containing children and most pets. Border hedges require care in trimming to keep the lowest parts

> The best security hedge
> is one made from spiny
> or thorny plants

furnished with healthy shoots. A well-made border hedge will provide a secure and impenetrable barrier.

The best security hedge is one made from spiny or thorny plants, and some of the most hostile are firethorns, hawthorns,

barberries, and some hollies. In many instances, a single-line hedge is sufficient, but other situations may require a more determined effort. Wire or wooden fencing between a double line of hedge plants reinforces a boundary, and when the plants mature, they will obscure the fence.

Immediate Borders

In situations where encroachment and immediate privacy is paramount, it will be necessary to erect an artificial fence, either permanently or as a short-term measure, while hedge plants establish themselves around it. Temporary structures are usually the cheaper option, and there is a wide range of materials to choose from. Where permanent fences must be erected, they can

SOLID BOUNDARY
This well-made and maintained yew hedge is highly ornamental, which supplements its effectiveness as a solid boundary. The fence and mix of hedge forms make an attractive perimeter, providing privacy and security.

◀ SUBTLE PERIMETER
Even a formal hedge is a softer boundary than a wall or fence, because its foliage picks up the greenery of plants inside and outside the garden.

▼ INVITING VIEW
The arch cut into this boundary hedge both frames the gate and leads the eye into the garden beyond.

be used to support climbers, especially roses, to form a barrier that is sometimes referred to as a fedge (*see p.7*). Alternatively, a line of shrubs may be planted against a fence on the garden side, which will eventually give the effect of a continuous hedge.

BORDERS FOR PRIVACY

Hedges established along a border give privacy by removing or reducing the influence of neighboring sites and activities, and they create a sense of isolation. It takes time, however, to attain sufficient thickness and height.

If your budget permits, position hedge plants very closely together, because this will give an effective density at the earliest possible time. Evergreen species ensure year-round privacy, although most deciduous kinds are perfectly adequate once they are well established. Probably the fastest growing hedge plant of all is the evergreen conifer Leyland cypress, but it must be carefully managed – overgrown specimens are a notorious source of strife between neighbors, so it is not an ideal choice for a small property. Other conifers make quick-growing hedges, including Monterey cypress and Western red cedar. Lawson cypress also makes a good boundary, although it is not quite as fast growing.

GOOD BORDER HEDGES

Crataegus monogyna (Singleseed hawthorn) Spiny hedge; white spring flowers; deciduous.

Escallonia rubra Fast-growing; excellent for coastal sites; several forms available; evergreen.

Fagus sylvatica (Common beech) Bright green foliage; retains crisp brown leaves into winter if trimmed in late summer; deciduous.

Prunus laurocerasus (Cherry laurel) Fast-growing, dense hedge; evergreen.

Ribes sanguineum (Flowering currant) Crimson spring flowers; deciduous.

Taxus baccata (English yew) Dark green foliage; for formal trimming; evergreen.

Thuja plicata (Western red cedar) One of the best conifers; relatively fast-growing; evergreen.

HEDGES AS SCREENS

AROUND MANY YARDS, the surrounding land presents annoyances or distractions. Traffic noise from an adjacent street, for example, can certainly restrict the enjoyment of a yard or garden, and the problem is amplified where moving traffic can also be seen. In this situation, a carefully made screening hedge can help, with the aim to develop a dense evergreen barrier that will mask the street, decorate the site, and protect from pollution.

NOISE AND AIR POLLUTION

Dense evergreen hedges are a useful way to reduce noise levels from nearby railroads and streets, although it must be kept in mind that a hedge is likely to only reduce noise rather than eliminate it altogether. Conifers are the best choices, and they are most effective where they are planted at least two rows deep.

The degree of sound deadening is directly influenced by the height, maturity, and density of a hedge, and particularly by the relative elevation of the noise source. It is much more difficult, for example, to avoid noise from a source above garden level than one at the same level. To improve their sound-proofing qualities, maintain hedges with the minimum of trimming.

Hedges planted for sound proofing are also known to interrupt the flow of chemically polluted air. In places where pollution levels are a concern – for example, children's play areas or vegetable and herb gardens that are close to a busy street – a dense hedge is probably the only effective form of protection available to gardeners.

In certain sites, it may be possible to construct a solid screen made from hardwood cuttings (*see pp.50–51*) of willow. A wall of soil is contained between two screens woven from the cuttings, which will take root at many points to produce a solid, living barrier. At the beginning of each growing season, the top and sides of the screen are pruned back hard to keep it in shape.

TALL SCREEN
This dense, evergreen Leyland cypress hedge obscures a neighboring brick building. It is an excellent, fast-growing hedge plant, but it must be contained by regular trimming.

◄ GREEN SCREEN
This dense mixed hedge is kept just high enough to screen a bare fence. The contrasting appeal of hedges and fences is evident here.

▼ BERRIED SCREEN
Cotoneaster lacteus *is one of the best evergreens for a formal or informal screen. Its scarlet berries ripen from autumn into winter.*

UNWANTED VIEWS

Vistas from a yard or garden may be spoiled by distant or nearby unattractive buildings, which are out of keeping with the surroundings. Planting a hedge as a living screen is a decorative way to blot out any eyesores. It is quite possible to keep sections of a hedge at different heights to obscure the objectionable and to include the agreeable elements of a view, such as elegant trees and attractive shrubs in neighboring land.

> A decorative hedge is a good way to screen an unattractive view

Within a yard, it is often desirable to screen certain utilitarian areas, such as trash cans or compost heaps. Here, hedges offer the ideal solution, particularly the ornamental, informal types that bear flowers and fruits. Living screens, or fedges, can also be made from wooden, metal, or brick structures that support climbing plants, like roses, or sweet peas and other annual flowers, or trained fruits, such as apples and pears, and blackberries and loganberries.

URBAN HEDGES

Hedges that tolerate urban pollution:
***Brachyglottis* 'Sunshine'** White-hairy leaves; bright yellow, daisylike flowers all summer.
Buxus microphylla (Small-leaved boxwood) Dark green leaves turn bronze in winter.
Mahonia aquifolium (Oregon grape) Dark green, spiny leaves turn red-purple in winter; yellow flowers in spring.
Olearia* × *haastii Dark green leaves; daisy-like flowers from midsummer; dense growth.
Pyracantha coccinea (Firethorn) Dark green foliage; creamy flowers in early summer.

HEDGES FOR SHELTER

AN EXTREMELY IMPORTANT REASON for creating a hedge is to provide garden protection from the wind. Strong winds can cause damage to buildings, greenhouses, and frames, and even moderate winds can loosen plant roots, break stems and shoots, and cause scorching of leaves. A garden enclosed by a hedge will form a sheltered microclimate, and plants perform better in such conditions than in an exposed, unprotected site.

SHELTER FROM WIND

The overwhelming reason to plant a hedge is to provide shelter from winds. Strong winds can cause physical damage to buildings and plants, and even a gentle breeze makes a garden cooler and drier as a result of increased loss of water and heat. In consequence, wind retards plant growth, from germination to early establishment and reduces chances of survival in cold winters. Useful pollinating activity by insects will be impaired; there may be greater heat loss from greenhouses; and spraying of plants with pesticides will be hindered. Where there is extreme exposure, especially in coastal areas, there may be soil erosion and damage to foliage from salt deposits or sand abrasion, the consequence of which is dramatic stunting of growth.

Wind striking a permeable barrier, such as a hedge, is filtered and calmed

The purpose of a shelter hedge is to filter rather than totally obstruct windflow. Wind striking a solid or near-solid barrier, like a wall or fence, is deflected upward over the

◀ SHELTER FROM SUN
Small areas of shade at the base of hedges present creative gardeners with the perfect opportunity to grow shade-loving plants, such as ferns.

HEDGES FOR EXPOSED SITES

Elaeagnus macrophylla Vigorous, spreading, evergreen growth; silvery green leaves.
Escallonia rubra Compact, evergreen growth; dark crimson to pink flowers in summer.
Fuchsia magellanica Deciduous shrub; hanging purple and red flowers in summer.
Hebe salicifolia Narrow, evergreen leaves; white or pale blue flowers until autumn.
Hydrangea macrophylla Deciduous; blue or pink summer flowerheads.
Olearia macrodonta (Daisy bush) Vigorous and evergreen; white daisy flowers in summer.
Quercus ilex (Holm oak) Rounded, evergreen growth; dark green foliage.
Tamarix pentandra Arching, deciduous growth; dense clusters of pink flowers in late summer.

WIND SHELTER
An established hedge brings invaluable wind shelter to a garden. This border of perennials thrives in the protected lee of a hornbeam hedge.

obstruction to create intense turbulence. A suction effect results to leeward, which can be even more damaging than the wind itself. So, plan for a reasonably open hedge.

Theoretically, the ideal permeability of a hedge is about 40 percent porosity. This is best obtained by deciduous species, but in practice even very dense evergreen hedges open up in windy conditions and effectively reduce wind velocity. As a rule, a mature hedge will usually offer shelter for a distance ten times its height to leeward.

SHADE AND SECLUSION

Hedges can provide another sort of shelter in gardens, for they often give welcome shade from hot sun in summer. Trained to a suitable height, hedges can be formed into attractive nooks or make sheltered spots for shade-loving plants.

Shade is often considered to present problems, but it provides contrast, which is essential in the well-designed garden. There are many plants, however, that thrive in or tolerate the shade of hedges. Ferns like the maidenhairs (*Adiantum*) and the soft shield fern (*Polystichum setiferum*) represent a valuable group, and hostas, bergenias, epimediums, lily-of-the-valley (*Convallaria majalis*), the Christmas and Lenten roses (*Helleborus*), cyclamens, and snowdrops (*Galanthus*) are all perennials reliable in shade. Shrubby plants for shade include camellias and skimmias, and there are climbers like ivy (*Hedera*) and clematis.

TRANQUIL SHELTER
Alluring nooks and crannies can be carved out of developing hedges, with judicious pruning, and furnished with garden seats.

HEDGES AS DIVIDERS AND BACKDROPS

CAREFULLY PLANTED, HEDGES can make a prominent contribution to garden design. In larger gardens, formally trimmed runs of one species of hedging provide dramatic effect, and they may be kept low or allowed to grow to their maximum manageable height. In any garden, it is often a good plan to add to a garden's overall interest by dividing the area up with several internal hedges clipped to different heights.

DIVISIONS AND UNITIES

Hedges can be skillfully used in garden design to divide a yard into distinct compartments, and this is a very effective method of making a small plot seem much larger than it actually is. The compartments may be defined in shape, such as circles, squares, or oblongs, and if they are planted to different themes of color or season, or with herbs or scented plants, interesting surprises and character are added to the yard. If there is room, some paving, a sculpture, or a small water feature can be added to complement the overall pattern.

The architectural qualities of formally trimmed hedges are sometimes used to lessen the stark contrast between a building and its environment. They extend the line of a house into the yard, allowing the home to blend with its garden setting. Informal hedges are equally valuable, but they will be more demanding of space.

HEDGE WITH A VIEW

To draw the eye to a special feature beyond a hedge, incorporate thoughtfully placed windows into a strong evergreen hedge, such as yew. A similar device is to cut an arched doorway into a tall hedge, which leads from one garden area to another. Hedge windows and doors require careful training and trimming during the early years of a hedge's development.

DRAMATIC PARTNERSHIP
English yew hedges divide this rose garden from other plantings; the dark yew foliage intensifies the impact of the vividly hued roses.

◄ A PERFECT FRAME
Instead of an arch or window, gaps cut into hedges perform the same function: to draw the eye to a special feature.

▼ EVERGREEN ARCH
This arch in a yew hedge allows people to stroll from one area of the garden to another.

Most evergreen conifers or hollies and the deciduous beech or hornbeam are suitable plants for hedge archways.

BEAUTIFUL BACKDROPS

Although island plantings of shrubs and herbaceous plants can be interesting and justified, their visual impact is much enhanced where they are planted in borders in front of an established and trimmed hedge, which provides a sympathetic backdrop. An evergreen species is the best

> Herbaceous borders are shown to best effect in front of a hedge

choice for this purpose, but remember to leave enough space between the hedge and the display plants to allow for access for trimming and also to reduce the effects of root competition.

Well-established evergreen hedge plants can be adorned by planting certain climbers with them. Good climbing partners include glory flower (*Eccremocarpus scaber*), canary creeper (*Tropaeolum peregrinum*), flame nasturtium (*Tropaeolum speciosum*), perennial pea (*Lathyrus latifolius*), and different types of large-flowered clematis.

INTERNAL HEDGE PLANTS

Buxus sempervirens (Boxwood) Small evergreen foliage needs regular clipping.
Camellia japonica Evergreen growth; variety of attractive spring flowers.
Euonymus japonicus (Japanese spindle) Evergreen; tolerates coastal or urban sites.
Forsythia × intermedia Decidous growth; masses of yellow flowers in spring.
Fuchsia magellanica Deciduous; suitable for seaside gardens; red and purple summer flowers.
Garrya elliptica (Silk-tassel bush) Evergreen; attractive silver-gray catkins in winter.
Lonicera nitida (Shrubby honeysuckle) Bushy evergreen; various attractive leaf forms.
***Spiraea* 'Arguta'** (Bridal wreath) Deciduous; clusters of white flowers in spring.

ORNAMENTAL HEDGES

THE HISTORY OF ORNAMENTAL HEDGING stretches back hundreds of years, and it gives modern-day gardeners plenty of inspiration to draw upon. Architecture is a common model for hedge design, often creating interesting shadows. Some hedges have an arch, recess, or window cut into them, and battlements or waves make an eye-catching alternative to a flat top. Then there is edging: low hedges clipped to form patterns within a garden or to border pathways and beds.

LOW HEDGES AND EDGING

Where a garden needs a defining edge or partition, but it is undesirable to obscure other parts of the yard, low hedges serve the purpose perfectly. Informally trained flowering species are a good choice here. Try plants like rosemary, *Brachyglottis* 'Sunshine', *Potentilla fruticosa*, English lavender, and *Perovskia atriplicifolia*; the last two are excellent when planted together. Low hedges planted along the borders of a pathway make very effective features.

Boxwood is a tried- and-tested plant for very low pathway edging, and there are several cultivated varieties with different leaf forms available. When it comes to forming the intricate shapes of a knot garden, boxwood is the front-runner of edging plants, although lavender cotton and wall germander are both low plants that suit the purpose well.

A very artistic form of design is to contain one or several garden beds within a formal pattern of edging. Even though this idea can be depicted in a garden of

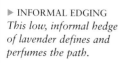

▲ ARTISTIC AND PRACTICAL
Beds of vegetables and herbs are bordered and protected here by a formal pattern of boxwood edging.

▶ INFORMAL EDGING
This low, informal hedge of lavender defines and perfumes the path.

◀ BOXWOOD TOPIARY
The top line of a formal hedge can be trimmed into unusual shapes, such as clouds or crenellations. Trimming requires time and patience, however; rounded shapes are the simplest to do.

small or medium size, it is best exhibited on a large scale in a spacious yard, and where it can be viewed from above.

TOPIARY HEDGES

To give your garden a distinct sense of character, be imaginative with the top line of a formal hedge. Instead of a straight line, trim it into castellations, undulations, or uneven cloud patterns. A rewarding challenge is to ornament the tops of

> Hedge topiary will give a garden a distinct sense of character

hedges with sculpted formal contours, in the form of balls, geometric shapes, or even imaginative representations of birds and animals. These features are known collectively as topiary.

The ancient crafts of topiary and hedge-making have long been closely associated, chiefly because they both require similar plants, and they share a common need for careful training and trimming.

Maintenance of topiary figures calls for regular, patient attention. Rounded shapes are the easiest to make and manage, while bird and animal shapes justify the painstaking effort involved by providing the greatest satisfaction and admiration.

Topiary figures need to be developed at well-spaced intervals, and they look particularly imposing if used to punctuate the ends of hedges. Alternatively, topiary figures can be grown independently but alongside a traditional formal or informal hedge to provide an appealing contrast.

LOW HEDGES

Berberis thunbergii Fresh green leaves redden in autumn; pale yellow flowers in spring.
Brachyglottis 'Sunshine' White-hairy leaves; bright yellow daisy flowers through summer.
Lonicera nitida (Shrubby honeysuckle) Tiny, dark green leaves; insignificant cream flowers.
Potentilla fruticosa Spreading, low hedge; yellow flowers from spring to autumn.
Rosmarinus officinalis (Rosemary) Aromatic leaves; blue flowers in spring and autumn.
Santolina chamaecyparissus (Lavender cotton) Gray leaves; yellow daisy flowers in late summer.
Teucrium chamaedrys (Wall germander) Dark leaves; red or pink flowers in summer.

THE CRAFT OF PLEACHING

For the dedicated gardener with a medium- to large-sized plot, the craft of pleaching is an absorbing challenge. The aim is to produce a hedge that consists of a row of trees that have their branches woven together to form a wall of shoots and leaves. Combined with formal trimming, it results in an outstanding ornamental hedge feature with an intricate branch structure on a freestanding row of clear trunks.

Pleaching, like topiary, is another long-established garden craft: in Tudor England, pleached avenues were status symbols, used to show off the number of gardeners a landowner was able to employ. Indeed, pleached hedges carry a high price for the modern gardener: the expenditure of much time training and pruning (*see p.47*).

Pleached rows and avenues are enjoying a revival today, despite the fact that they require almost constant attention throughout their lives. The trees most

---

A strong, well-made framework is needed for a pleached hedge

---

traditionally used for this form of pruning are linden (*Tilia*), hornbeam, and common beech. A strong and well-constructed framework will be needed until the row is fully established, which may be nearly 15 years for hornbeam and common beech. In some situations, it may be possible to create a pleached tunnel by planting two rows of

PLEACHED LINDENS
A pleached row of trees results in a free-standing hedge that is lifted clear of the ground on a row of trunks. A pleached hedge requires time-consuming skill in formation and maintenance, so this is for the dedicated gardener only.

trees side by side. When the trees are tall enough, the tops of each row can be trained together so that they join in the middle to form an arching roof.

HEDGES FOR MAZES

A review of ornamental hedges would be incomplete without mention of the maze, a traditional puzzle of pathways contained by trimmed hedges. The most usual concept is a large-scale planting where the hedges are grown up to 6ft (2m) high so that it is not possible to observe an exit route. Such mazes are suited only to extensive garden sites and are commonly made of evergreens, such as yews, hollies, western red cedars, and cypresses. More suitable as a design feature for medium-sized gardens are mazes formed from low-growing edging shrubs, especially boxwood. Here, a confusion of bordered pathways is developed as a form of knot garden, which can be readily admired from above. Although miniature hedges require regular clipping, even small layouts can be effective.

STAGGERED BLOCKS
This network of formal paths and hedges mixes maze-type features with those of an elaborate garden. It makes a beautifully puzzling design, yet there is no problem with getting lost.

GOOD FORMAL HEDGES

Buxus sempervirens **'Suffruticosa'** Variety of boxwood with bright green new growth.

Chamaecyparis lawsoniana (Lawson cypress) Dense sprays of evergreen, aromatic foliage; forms with different foliage colours exist.

Corylus avellana (European hazel) Green leaves turn yellow in autumn before falling; hanging yellow catkins in spring.

Crataegus laevigata (English hawthorn) Glossy, deciduous leaves; thorny branches.

Elaeagnus macrophylla Glossy, evergreen leaves with silvery undersides.

Lonicera nitida (Shrubby honeysuckle) Small and glossy, evergreen leaves; fast-growing.

Sorbus intermedia (Swedish whitebeam) Dark green, deciduous foliage.

Taxus baccata (English yew) Dark, evergreen foliage; female plants bear red fruits.

Thuja plicata (Western red cedar) Dark green, aromatic sprays of evergreen foliage.

FLOWERING HEDGES

A HEDGE CAN BE MADE from almost any species of flowering garden shrub if several specimens are planted together in a continuous line. Choice is led by personal preferences, manageability, and cost, but it is sensible to concentrate first thoughts on plants that are well tried as hedges. Flowering hedges are well suited to situations where a dividing feature is needed in the garden, or where a period of flowering adds to the interest of a backdrop or screening hedge.

AN EXTENDED RANGE

The majority of cultivated woody plants are available in a variety of forms, either selected from wild specimens or as a result of breeding. These plants extend the range of choice, but it is important to get advice on the vigor and sturdiness of particular cultivated varieties. Some choice selections do not relish containment as hedges.

INFORMALITY AND FLOWERING

To be seen at their best, flowering hedges need to be grown informally, which means that they are regularly and carefully pruned while maintaining much of their natural habit (see p.45). Excellent flowering evergreens, such as the many species and cultivars of camellias, Mexican orange blossoms, and silk- tassel bushes are among plants relatively more orderly in their habit than the good deciduous flowering hedges, such as abelias, deutzias, fuchsias, common brooms, and mock

> ### Flowering hedges need to be grown informally to be seen at their best

oranges. Informal hedges invariably take up more space than formally trained ones, but trimming to shape does not necessarily mean loss of bloom. Escallonias, olearias, viburnums, witch hazels, firethorns, flowering quinces, and forsythias will all bear flowers on shoots clipped to a restricted hedge shape.

LOW FLOWERS
This compact shrub,
Potentilla fruticosa
'Vilmoriniana',
makes a suitable low flowering hedge, bearing saucer-shaped yellow flowers through summer. Many different colored flower forms of Potentilla fruticosa *exist, and they are suitable as informal flowering hedges.*

◄ FLOWERING
BORDER
*Flowering quince is a
deciduous flowering
shrub that can be
clipped to a formal
shape, but the best
display of flowers is
seen when the plant
is kept informally. It
also has sharp thorns,
which makes it a
good border hedge.*

▼ SPRING COLOR
Berberis darwinii
*bears hanging clusters
of dark orange
flowers in profusion
throughout spring.
They are followed by
blue-black berries. It
can be kept as a semi-
formal hedge.*

COLOR THROUGH THE SEASONS

It is possible to plan sections of a garden
to contain hedges that offer flowering
interest for progressive months. Winter-
flowering hedges can brighten short days,
and many are also fragrant. They should
be established in close proximity to the
house so that they may be enjoyed at
close range from inside. White-flowered
laurustinus (*Viburnum tinus*) does well
over a wide area and in shade, and various
witch hazels make attractive deciduous
barriers with starlike flowers borne
on the bare branches. Winter jasmine
(*Jasminum nudiflorum*) and *Lonicera
fragrantissima* both form useful winter-
flowering hedges. Not always appreciated
as flowers are the winter and early spring
catkins of the silk- tassel bush, European
hazel, and willow.

Spring-flowering plants suitable for in-line planting include various types of barberries, amelanchiers, camellias, ceanothus, kerrias, flowering quinces, forsythias, osmanthus, flowering currants, and spiraeas. Even this short selection represents the diversity of plants that can be grown as hedges: there are evergreen and deciduous choices, some with spines, some with colored stems or fruits, and some that offer the spectacle of autumn color.

Summer flowering hedges can be made from numerous garden shrubs, such as the low-growing *Brachyglottis* 'Sunshine' with its bright yellow daisy flowers and gray leaves, the white-flowered Mexican orange blossom, and the many cultivars of hydrangeas and grevilleas. Also of interest in summer are well-known garden favorites like deutzias, escallonias, hebes, olearias, mock oranges, and weigelas – all of these are commonly seen in the shrub border, but they are also suitable candidates for an informal hedge planting.

LIGHT BLUE LACECAPS
Lacecap hydrangeas, like H. macrophylla 'Mariesii Perfecta' above, make fine hedges; equally suitable are the mophead types.

FRAGRANT HEDGES

Escallonia 'Apple Blossom' Rich pink flowers in early summer; evergreen foliage.
Lavandula angustifolia (English lavender) Dense spikes of fragrant, pale to deep purple flowers from midsummer; evergreen leaves.
Lonicera fragrantissima Creamy white flowers in winter and early spring; deciduous foliage.
Mahonia japonica Pale yellow flowers in arching clusters from late autumn; evergreen.
Myrtus communis (Common myrtle) Whiskery white flowers in early autumn; evergreen.
Osmanthus heterophyllus Tubular white flowers from late summer; evergreen foliage.
Philadelphus 'Belle Etoile' White flowers with purple centers in early summer; deciduous.
Rosa CONSTANCE SPRY ('Austance') Shrub rose with pink summer flowers; deciduous foliage.
Rosmarinus officinalis (Rosemary) tubular purple-blue flowers in early summer; evergreen.

For a longer-lasting summer display that continues until autumn, consider species and cultivated varieties of abelias, fuchsias, hibiscus, myrtles, and potentillas. It may also be possible to extend the seasonal interest of a flowering hedge if it is made up of a variety of species that bloom at different times of year. However, the ornamental effect of a flowering hedge is usually much more effective where a run of the same plant is established.

ROSE HEDGES

Many roses are suitable as summer-flowering hedges. There are a number of distinctive groups of rose, however, and the following selection will narrow the choice.

From the old garden roses, consider plants in the alba, gallica, and sweet briar groups. The albas make large plants with few spines and bear clusters of double or semidouble, fragrant flowers; *Rosa alba* 'Maxima' is a choice, white-flowered example. Gallicas have a dense, prolific habit with usually spiny stems on which clusters of three single or double, strongly scented flowers are borne. There are many different colored varieties from which to choose, of which R. 'Duc de Guiche' is a crimson-purple example. The sweet briars are vigorous, dense plants with spiny stems and fragrant, single or double

Fragrance is all too often forgotten – choose a rose hedge for its scent

flowers, which are carried either singly or in clusters; R. *rubiginosa* represents this group, and there are numerous selections.

The modern garden roses contain many suitable hedging subjects in the floribunda, polyantha, rugosa, shrub, and rambler groups. The floribundas are continuous flowerers that come in great variety – upright or bushy – with single or double, lightly scented flowers borne in clusters of up to twenty-four. The polyanthas, such as the white R. 'Katharina Zeimet', are compact plants with few spines, and here again flowers come in great variety, although they are rarely scented. Rugosas have very spiny stems with tough leaves, and they produce fragrant, single or semidouble flowers in clusters of up to twelve. The shrub rose group includes a great variety of interesting types that mostly grow up to 6ft (2m); the stems are often thorny, and the flowers usually scented. Rambling roses may be established on a low support structure to form a useful barrier or screen. This is sometimes described as a fedge (*see p.7*).

▲ SILKY TASSELS
Not always appreciated as a flowering plant Garrya elliptica *bears its silvery catkins in winter and spring. It has an orderly shape that can be kept as a semiformal hedge.*

◄ SEASONAL GLORY
The tidy, robust habit of spiraeas (here, S. japonica *'Anthony Waterer') make them suitable as informal spring- and summer-flowering hedge plants.*

Fruiting Hedges

THE SMALLER THE GARDEN, the more important the choice of hedging plants. Well worthy of consideration are those specimens that not only form an effective hedge but also bear ornamental fruits. This is a bonus characteristic, just as plants are selected for their foliage or flowers. Some hedges possess a range of ornamental features, like English hawthorn, which has white spring flowers, red fruit in autumn, and lobed leaves.

A RANGE OF COLORS

Besides English hawthorn, mentioned above, there are other thorny hedge species that redeem their hostility with interesting fruits, such as flowering quince, firethorn, and the hardy orange. These and other fruits exist in a range of colors from the glossy red berries of the Japanese laurel through the purple-black berries of the black elder to the white of fruits of snowberry plants. The strawberry tree is noted for its unusually textured, dull red fruits, although it makes an expensive choice for hedging.

The finest fruiting hedges are those where the leaves and fruits combine well; for example, the berries of both common holly and *Cotoneaster salicifolius*

▲ BLUE HOLLY
The bluish green leaves of Ilex × meserveae *selections give these vigorous hollies their name. They contrast well with the glossy berries.*

◀ FIRETHORN
Pyracanthas are popular for their spiny branches and bright berries.

ESPALIERED APPLE
This apple tree has been trained along a wire support into a shape known as an espalier. It can be grown as a hedge that flowers in spring and yields an edible crop at the end of summer.

'Rothschildianus' contrast well with their leaves. Be aware that berried plants can become weeds outside their native environment, however, when birds disperse the seeds.

Many plants contain chemicals that are poisonous to humans and animals, and in some cases these are concentrated in the fruits. Young children are most at risk from plant poisoning because they frequently

> Fruiting hedges attract wildlife to a garden, especially birds

put things in their mouths, and berries are especially attractive. Children must be taught that if a plant is not a recognized food it should not be eaten. All of the plants mentioned so far are quite safe to grow, so long as they are treated as ornamentals and not food.

HEDGES WITH EDIBLE FRUIT

Any reference to fruiting hedges should not overlook cultivated fruit. A neatly managed row of raspberries, blackberries,

or loganberries, and apples, pears, or peaches trained as cordons or espaliers, can make excellent dividers or screens. A thoughtfully planned grouping can give year-round interest.

Fruiting hedges will certainly attract wildlife to a garden, especially birds, and valued fruit may need netted protection. No doubt there will be conflicts of interest, but most gardeners are prepared to share their yards with nature's visitors.

HEDGES WITH FRUITS

Berberis thunbergii Glossy red fruits; fresh green foliage turns orange-red in autumn.
Chaenomeles speciosa (Flowering quince) Aromatic, green-yellow fruits; glossy foliage.
Cotoneaster frigidus 'Cornubia' Abundant red fruits; dark green foliage.
Crataegus crus-galli (Cockspur hawthorn) Long-lasting deep red fruits; dark green leaves.
Ilex × altaclerensis Scarlet berries in abundance; bright green leaves.
Photinia glabra Spherical red fruits turn to black; dark green foliage.
Pyracantha coccinea (Firethorn) Profuse red berries; dark green leaves; spiny branches.
Rhamnus alaternus (Italian buckthorn) Red fruits ripen to black; dark green foliage.
Rosa moyesii Large, bottle-shaped, orange-red hips; mid- to dark green leaves.

LEAVES AND STEMS

THE CHARACTERISTICS OF LEAVES AND STEMS offer added attraction to hedge plants, often complementing any attributes of flowers and fruits. The range of leaf shape and size is very great and gives the opportunity to introduce a variety of hedging texture to the garden scene: some bold, some subtle. From the dark hue of yew through the mid-green of mock orange and the bright green of *Kerria japonica*, green leaves come in different shades, too.

LEAF COLOR AND TEXTURE

Many good hedge plants have red-, purple-, and yellow-leaved forms, including European hazel, common beech, cherry plum (*Prunus cerasifera*), whitebeam (*Sorbus aria*), and *Pittosporum tenuifolium*; some conifers have yellow forms.

Interesting foliage variants are also seen in Japanese spindles, mock oranges, spireas, and weigelas. Gray, a restful color, is well represented among hedge subjects, many of which make good low hedges. Consider

> A length of red-leaved hedging is striking near others of green or gray

wall germander, *Brachyglottis* 'Sunshine', *Elaeagnus macrophylla*, sea buckthorn, English lavender, and lavender cotton. A length of red-leaved hedging makes a striking effect near others of green or gray.

Every list of possible choices should contain plants with autumn color. The shadbush (*Amelanchier canadensis*) turns rich red as leaf fall approaches, and the

▲ TWO-TONE LEAVES
Consider variegated forms for hedge plants, such as Elaeagnus × ebbingei *'Gilt Edge', above.*

▶ MIXED WINTER TEXTURES
The glossy, evergreen leaves of common holly mix well with clipped hornbeam, which keeps its crisp brown, desiccated leaves all through winter.

◄ PRIZE PLUM
Prunus cerasifera 'Nigra' is a purple-leaved form of the dark green myrobolan. Pink flowers appear in early spring on the bare branches.

▼ WINTER CHEER
The bright yellow stems of Cornus stolonifera *'Flaviramea' are ideal for winter color. It makes a low hedge if pruned hard each year.*

leaves of witch hazels become yellow. Common beech and hornbeam hedges retain their crisp autumn leaves through winter; they are finally shed in spring.

The flattened sprays of scalelike leaves borne on conifers such as Leyland cypress and western red cedar are quite different from the broad leaves of flowering hedge shrubs such as hydrangeas, and the large leaves of Japanese laurel contrast with the small foliage of common broom or boxwood. Leaf texture plays a vital role in garden design, so choose carefully.

ATTRACTIVE STEMS
With their unmistakable shoots, bamboos make graceful screens, but beware – they are notorious invaders; fountain bamboo (*Fargesia nitida*) is probably the best for small to medium gardens. Better behaved are the dogwoods, *Cornus alba* and

C. stolonifera both have colorful stems and they can be made to form low hedges if they are cut back annually. Himalayan honeysuckle presents attractive green stems to supplement its flowers, and for an unusual hedging subject try the twisted, corkscrew-like form of European hazel, *Corylus avellana* 'Contorta'.

AROMATIC FOLIAGE

Juniperus chinensis Strongly scented sprays of dark green foliage; evergreen conifer.
Laurus nobilis (Bay laurel) Aromatic, dark green, oval leaves, can be used as a flavoring in cooking; evergreen.
Myrtus communis (Common myrtle) Scented, dark green leaves; evergreen.
Perovskia atriplicifolia Finely cut and deeply divided, aromatic, gray-green leaves; deciduous.
Rosmarinus officinalis (Rosemary) Strongly aromatic, white-felty, dark leaves; evergreen.

LOOKING AFTER HEDGES

CHOOSING AND BUYING HEDGES

HEDGE PLANTS ARE AVAILABLE EITHER as bare-root transplants or, more usually, as container-grown plants. Bare-root specimens are freshly dug from the nursery bed, and hedge plants that are easy to raise from seed, such as hawthorn and beech, or new plants from cuttings are frequently handled in this way. For a hedge, choose young plants, because there is less likely to be a check in growth, and the roots will establish more vigorously.

CHOOSING HEALTHY HEDGES

Bare-root hedge plants are invariably cheaper than those sold in containers, and they can often be bought by mail order or directly from the nursery. They must have sturdy root systems and not be badly damaged or excessively pruned. Container-grown plants are best inspected carefully before purchase. Like bare-root plants, their tops must be undamaged and healthy, but most importantly, there should be good root development. To check the rootball, invert a specimen and remove its container.

BUYING TIPS

- Bare-root plants usually come in bundles, and they must be bought and planted in their dormant season.
- Container-grown specimens can be bought for planting at any time of year, even though the dormant season is the best time to plant.
- Superior plants are more likely to be found in garden outlets where the turnover of sales is high.
- Plants offered very cheaply might be of poor quality.
- Most garden centers and specialist outlets have high standards, with trained staff on hand to offer advice.

Robust and healthy, closely branched top-growth shows no sign of pests or diseases

Rootball is well developed and shows no evidence of being pot-bound

WHAT TO LOOK FOR
Container-grown plants must be carefully checked before purchase. The roots should have explored the growing medium thoroughly without being pot-bound or showing signs of very recent potting.

◀ LONG-LASTING INVESTMENT *A well-maintained hedge repays with years of splendor.*

How to Plant a Hedge

For hedge plants to establish well, there must be minimal disruption to growth as they are moved from one growing environment to another. Planting specimens while they are dormant reduces disturbance, but in all cases it is most important to see that the hedge site is well prepared so that it encourages early growth. Ground already in cultivation presents few challenges; establishing a hedge in a regularly mown area of grass is generally easy and straightforward.

Clearing a Site of Weeds

Sites colonized by perennial weeds must be dealt with long before planting. Weeds compete with hedges for food and water, and if they become established in a hedge, they are unsightly and difficult to remove.

The simplest way to clear a weedy site is to use a spade and fork. Mechanical rotary cultivators can be used for large areas, but this method needs to be combined with hand forking and possibly weedkiller.

CLEARING WEEDS WITH A FORK
Systematic forking out of perennial weeds is best done in summer when warm weather assists by drying out and killing exposed roots.

TACKLING PERSISTENT WEEDS
Some perennial weeds are persistent and difficult to eradicate. Combine hand forking with repeated applications of weedkiller.

WEEDKILLERS

• The most environmentally satisfactory means of weeding is by cultivating; on heavily infested sites, however, weedkillers may be necessary.

• Very effective chemical weedkillers are available, but to justify their cost and to ensure success, be sure to follow the instructions with regard to susceptible weeds, timing, dosage, and risk to valued plants nearby.

MANURES AND FERTILIZERS

If a hedge is to be planted on a site that has been in successful garden cultivation, there is no need to add any manures or fertilizers to the soil; in fact, this may actually discourage hedge plant roots from exploring deeply. On sandy soils or sites of poor water-holding capacity, however, it is sensible to incorporate well-rotted compost or animal manure into the base of the preparation trench (*see opposite, top*). Similarly, supplementary fertilizers are necessary only on less fertile sites, where a dressing of general fertilizer will suffice.

WELL-ROTTED MANURE

PREPARING THE SITE

The hedge planting site must be carefully prepared since this is an essential step toward good plant establishment. It is an important way to remove any competitive weeds that remain in the ground, and it aerates the soil, which ensures good drainage and the encouragement of strong roots as early as possible. On sites that are not suitably fertile, it also provides an opportunity to incorporate organic manure and fertilizer (*see opposite, below*).

To prepare your site, dig a spade-deep trench about 12in (30cm) wide across one end of the intended planting strip and remove the soil to a pile at the opposite end. Dig a second trench next to the first, inverting the soil into the first trench. Continue the process progressively to the end of the planting strip. The pile of soil taken from the first trench is used to fill the last trench. Aim to complete site preparation a month or two before planting to allow the soil to settle.

DIGGING TIPS

• In frost-prone areas, clay soils are best dug in autumn; winter's cold makes a good tilth by shattering large clods through freeze-thaw action.

• Organic matter and fertilizers can be added to the soil during its preparation, if necessary.

• Well-drained, sandy soils can be dug at most times of year; add manure or compost to improve retention of moisture and nutrients (*see opposite, below*).

1 **Mark out the edge** of the hedge site with a garden line. Dig a trench to a depth of one spade blade; the method described above is easiest.

2 **Move the line** to the center of the dug area and insert stakes at measured intervals along this line to mark where the plants are to go (*see p.39*).

PLANTING INTO GRASS

Where a hedge is to be planted into grass, this should be first mown short or destroyed with a nonpersistent weedkiller. Skim the surface to a depth of 2in (5cm), in strips 12×12in (30×30cm), and invert these turf layers into the trench as digging proceeds (*see above*). The turf layers must be chopped into small pieces so that they do not form an impermeable layer, which may impede drainage. Perennial grass weeds, such as quack grass, should not be skimmed in this way; carefully remove them by forking out.

LIFTING TURF
Undercut the turf with a spade to 2in (5cm) deep. Each section should be about 12in (30cm) wide.

RECYCLING THE TURF
The turf that has been lifted is inverted and chopped up at the bottom of the planting trench, where it will rot down.

PUTTING IN HEDGE PLANTS

The rules relating to the planting of hedge specimens are similar to those for any tree or shrub. Plants set out in late autumn will establish at the very start of the next growing season, and spring planting is preferable in very exposed situations to avoid winter weather damage, but beware of droughts in spring or early summer. All bare-root specimens must be planted in winter, and those grown in containers are best planted at a similar time; it is risky to plant them when in full growth. If planting is temporarily delayed, set the plants into a hole and cover their roots with moist, loose soil. Never attempt to plant when the ground is frozen. If plants are received at such a time, store them intact under cover until the planting site is workable.

1 **Dig planting holes** at sites marked with stakes (*see p.37*). Be sure the holes are large enough to receive the existing roots without the need to constrict or prune them – about twice the width of a plant's rootball.

2 **Water plants thoroughly** before they are planted (here, *Ilex aquifolium*). If the rootball is allowed to dry out, it is more likely to be difficult to wet after planting, which is a frequent cause of losses.

3 **Place one hand** on top of the potting soil or mix and around the main stem of the plant to support it. Turn the plant upside down and with the other hand, carefully remove the container. Gently tease apart the roots at the base to encourage them to grow outward into the soil. Place the plant into the hole.

4 Be sure the hole is a similar depth to that of the rootball. With bare-root plants, the hole should be deep enough to accommodate the roots at the same depth as they were in the nursery bed – look for the soil mark.

5 Return the soil to the planting hole. With bare-root plants, gently shake the plant up and down to make sure the soil settles around the roots. Unless the soil is heavy and wet, firm around the roots with your foot.

6 The finished line of hedge plants should be left unstaked, unless they are on a very exposed site. The best plan in this case is to tie plants to the upwind side of a continuous wire. Staking can be detrimental in most other cases, because it prevents plants from flexing in the wind, which strengthens their roots.

PLANTING DISTANCES

For most gardens, a single line of hedge plants is sufficient and all that can be accommodated. The exception is where a very dense barrier of conifers is needed to reduce traffic noise. Here, plants can be established in a staggered, double row. Planting distances vary with the species and purpose, a decision often influenced by cost. Generally, the closer the plants are set apart, the quicker the hedge will establish.

SINGLE PLANTING
For most species, planting distances of 2–3ft (60–90cm) are usually satisfactory. Expensive subjects can be set more widely apart.

DOUBLE PLANTING
Inexpensive plants can be set 12in (30cm) or less apart. Staggered rows make up a hedge quickly where there is sufficient room.

ESTABLISHMENT AND AFTERCARE

MAKING AND MAINTAINING A HEDGE is an expensive undertaking, so the best of attention must be paid to its establishment and aftercare. Where single specimen trees and shrubs fail in a garden, they can usually be replaced without great difficulty, but the options are quite different for a hedge. In this case, failure of individual plants or runs of plants will be unsightly, and it may destroy the beneficial effects of a hedge.

WATERING A NEW HEDGE

Newly planted hedges are very susceptible to drought, particularly in spring and summer and on sandy soils. Begin with the essential soaking at planting time (*see right*), then water the plants at regular intervals, unless there has been abundant rainfall. Adequate water is vital for plant growth.

Hedge plants must always be given a thorough drenching, applied evenly and gently from a hose, watering can, or low-level drip irrigation system. If time can be found to do so on warm days, mist over the foliage early in the morning and once again late in the evening.

WATERING INTO A BASIN
On planting, draw up a very shallow wall of soil around the base of each plant. Water will collect here, and filter down to the roots.

APPLYING A MULCH

The value of a mulch put down on the soil surface after planting cannot be over-emphasized. Mulches not only reduce evaporation of water from the soil but also suppress weeds and improve the growing environment by preventing extreme fluctuations in soil temperature.

Well-rotted manure or compost make ideal mulching materials and should be spread 2–3in (5–8cm) deep over the planting strip immediately after it has been planted. Shredded bark and other materials, such as cocoa shells, are effective options, although they may begin to look messy if disturbed by wind, birds, and other animals.

RAKING OVER THE MULCH
It is best to apply mulch to moist soil. Keep mulch away from the base of the plants because it can cause them to rot.

INITIAL PRUNING

Careful pruning after planting will assist the early growth of formal hedges, ensuring branches down to ground level. Hawthorn, privet, and tamarisk are examples of species that benefit from cutting back to about 4in (10cm) after planting. Most deciduous species should have their overall size reduced by about one-third, which is best done after autumn planting or in the autumn following spring planting. Conifers, most evergreens, and informal hedge plants should not be cut back right after planting; in these cases any pruning is best left until there is good growth, usually after one growing season.

HARD PRUNING
Cutting back hard immediately after planting is a suitable treatment for privet (above), tamarisk, blackthorn, and hawthorn.

CREATING A BARRIER

New hedges planted in country areas may require protection from grazing animals, such as rabbits or woodchucks. A temporary, small-mesh wire net fence is the best defense, buried 4–6in (10–15cm) deep to deter burrowing. On windy sites, any close-knit barrier will help establish a hedge by reducing water loss from plants and soil.

1 **Drive a stake** firmly into the soil using a sledge-hammer. The top of the stake should be at least 6in (15cm) above the tops of the plants.

2 **Place additional** stakes along the length of the hedge. Attach fine netting to each stake by hammering in metal staples. Make sure the netting is tight and well secured.

3 **The finished wind barrier** must be at least 24in (60cm) away from the hedge, on its windward side. From time to time, make sure that the netting is still secure. Where burrowing animals are a problem, wire netting can be buried 4–6in (10–15cm) deep in the soil.

SHAPING, TRIMMING, AND PRUNING

WELL-GROOMED HEDGES make pleasing and interesting features. Neglected hedges invariably become straggly and less effective, and they may begin to obstruct views, pathways, or other plants. Formative pruning continues until the hedge reaches its final proportions; from then on, most informal hedges benefit from annual pruning, and a neat formal hedge will need regular clipping.

TOOLS FOR THE JOB

Whether to use hand shears or a powered hedge trimmer depends mostly on the scale of the task and on the time available. Hand shearing may be slower, but it gives an excellent effect if carefully done, especially for topiary work, and it involves much less noise and concentration. Saws and loppers are often needed for renovation work (*see pp.48–49*). Keep all cutting tools clean and sharp, and all moving parts regularly oiled.

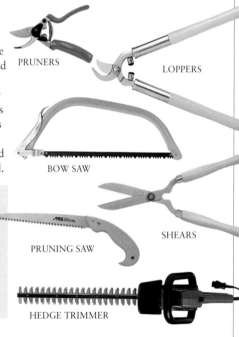

PRUNERS

LOPPERS

BOW SAW

PRUNING SAW

SHEARS

HEDGE TRIMMER

CHOOSING TOOLS

• Hand shears should be well balanced and not too heavy. For long runs of hedging, shears with long handles may be preferred.
• Electric trimmers are lighter and less noisy than those that run on gas. Never use them in wet conditions, and always connect them to a properly grounded outlet.
• Wear eye protectors when hedge cutting.

FORMATIVE PRUNING

Given good site preparation, hedge plants should grow away strongly in the year after planting; then, it will be necessary to begin a course of formative pruning. The few subjects that are best cut back hard immediately after planting (*see p.41*) should have the subsequent season's growth reduced by about a half to encourage a branching structure. Plants recommended for shortening by one-third after planting (*see p.41*) – the largest group of hedge plants – should have the leading shoot cut back and all sideshoots lightly trimmed. Do not cut conifers at all until the plants reach the required hedge height.

Trim the main stem back by at least two-thirds

Shorten all side-shoots by a half to an outward-facing bud

Remove crossing branches

ENCOURAGING A BRANCHING HABIT
Establishing strong lower branches is an important part of formative pruning; dominant upper branches should be trimmed back.

SHAPING A FORMAL HEDGE

Careful attention is needed to ensure that the progressive trimming of formal hedges leads to a profile that is wider at the base than at the top. This gives a hedge increased stability and prevents shading at the base, which could lead to unsightly bareness. Combined with a pointed or rounded top, a hedge with sloping sides is also less vulnerable to being pulled apart by the weight of any accumulated snow.

FLATTENED TOP
This yew hedge has been cut to a formal A-shape with a flat top. The tapering sides allow light to reach its lower growth.

POINTED SHAPE
This hornbeam hedge has been shaped to a pointed top, which discourages heavy snow from settling.

TRIMMING TIPS

• Begin by cutting back small areas at intervals along the hedge. They make reference points to work toward.
• With hand shears, try to cut with a continual, rhythmic motion.
• With a power trimmer, make smooth, sweeping cuts. Use the whole length of the blade.
• It is often more convenient to start trimming from the bottom of the hedge. Stand back occasionally to assess how straight you are cutting and the overall finish.

USING A SHAPING FRAME

If you find trimming a hedge by eye difficult, use jig frames made to the intended profile. These are erected over a developing hedge and connected by taut strings, which run along the length of the hedge as guidelines. Alternatively, cut the top of a hedge along a single string marker, then use a template to achieve the final profile (*see below*). Whatever method is used, keep the base as narrow as possible, but always wider than the top.

1 **Stretch a taut,** level string between the upright posts to act as a guideline for the highest point of the hedge. Cut the top of the hedge along this line.

2 **Cut a wooden** template to the shape required, and place it on the hedge. Cut along the line of the template, moving it along as you proceed.

3 **Remove the template** once you reach the end of the hedge, as well as the posts and line. Clip the ends of the hedge neatly, and clean up any bits you may have missed.

TRIMMING A FORMAL HEDGE

The most effective formal hedges are those trimmed frequently. Cutting stimulates shoot growth, and the skill is to cut shoots just beyond the basic structure. Most popular hedge plants really do benefit from several trims each growing season – done in late spring, midsummer, and autumn – although most species, including dwarf boxwood edging, respond well to two trims: one in midsummer, another in autumn. English lavender should be trimmed once after flowering. Some formal hedge plants, such as oleaster and cherry laurel, are better pruned just once, in autumn.

CUTTING WITH PRUNERS
Formal hedges with large leaves, such as holly and bay laurel, should never be sheared. This will shred the leaves giving an unsightly finish. Cut the shoots back with pruners.

TRIMMING WITH HAND SHEARS
Where the length of planting is modest, formal hedges with small leaves can be trimmed with hand shears. Keep the blades of the shears as parallel as possible to the hedge surface.

USING A HEDGE TRIMMER
When using a powered hedge trimmer, adopt a smooth, regular action with wide, sweeping cuts engaging the entire length of the cutter bar. Always wear eye protection and gloves.

WHEN TO TRIM

LATE SPRING, MIDSUMMER, AND AUTUMN
×*Cupressocyparis leylandii* (Leyland cypress)
Crataegus (Hawthorn)
Ligustrum (Privet)
Lonicera nitida (Shrubby honeysuckle)
Prunus spinosa (Blackthorn)

MIDSUMMER AND AUTUMN
Buxus sempervirens (Common boxwood)
Carpinus betulus (Hornbeam)
Chamaecyparis lawsoniana (Lawson cypress)
Escallonia
Fagus sylvatica (Common beech)
Ilex (Holly)
Taxus (Yew)

AUTUMN ONLY
Elaeagnus (Oleaster)
Lavandula angustifolia (English lavender)
Prunus laurocerasus (Cherry laurel)

Pruning Informal Hedges

Informal hedges have a free habit and demand less attention than formal hedges to make a good garden feature, although they do need more space. One pruning per season is usually sufficient to maintain neat growth and a good succession of flowers and fruits. Pruning of an informal hedge requires an understanding of the plant's growth habit, especially if the species bears flowers, fruits, or colorful stems. Some general guidelines are described below. In addition to pruners and loppers, a sharp pruning saw or bow saw may sometimes be necessary (*see p.42*).

GROUP 1: PRUNING AFTER FLOWERING
Plants that flower on wood produced in the previous growing season should be pruned soon after flowering so that new growth can develop in time for the next season. Remove about one-third of older shoots at the base.

WHEN TO PRUNE

Abelia × *grandiflora* Group 1.
Arbutus unedo (Strawberry tree) Group 3.
Berberis (Barberry) Group 1.
Brachyglottis 'Sunshine' Group 2.
Camellia Group 3.
Chaenomeles (Japonica) Group 1.
Cornus stolonifera (Red osier) Group 2.
Escallonia Group 1.
Forsythia × *intermedia* Group 1.
Fuchsia Group 2.
Leycesteria formosa Group 2.
Perovskia atriplicifolia Group 2.
Philadelphus (Mock orange) Group 1.
Potentilla fruticosa Group 3.
Pyracantha coccinea (Firethorn) Group 3.
Ribes sanguineum (Flowering currant) Group 2.
Rosmarinus officinalis (Rosemary) Group 3.
Salix (Willow) Group 2.

GROUP 2: HARD PRUNING IN SPRING
Plants that flower on shoots produced in the current season, or where colorful stems are a particular feature, should be pruned back hard in spring. It follows that this group is not suitable for situations where a screen is required all year round.

GROUP 3: INFREQUENT PRUNING
Evergreens, such as camellias and firethorns, and deciduous species that flower on side shoots and spurs are best not pruned regularly. Deadheading is helpful, and any cutting necessary to thin out congested shoots or to stimulate growth is best done after flowering.

MAINTAINING A TALL HEDGE

It is advisable to keep a hedge below 8ft (2.5m) tall, which is a manageable height that can be trimmed from ground level. Over-reaching is very tiring and can be dangerous. Where it is necessary to work above ground level, use lightweight ladders or steps and be sure they stand securely. If you use a scaffold, be especially careful.

TALL HEDGE TRIMMER
Extendable hedge trimmers are available for the maintenance of tall hedges.

SMALL SCAFFOLD
For very tall hedges, a trestle and plank structure can be used. For safe use, continuous concentration is essential. At least two adults will be needed to move the structure.

TOPIARY FOR FORMAL HEDGES

Topiary shapes require regular and precise clipping with hand shears. Fancy shapes, such as bird or animal forms, need a guide frame from the outset, which can be left in place as the hedge grows. Where necessary, shoots should be tied down with soft twine, which will eventually rot away. Rounded topiary pieces are usually cut freehand and are easier to produce and maintain than sharp-edged geometric shapes. Many plants are suitable, typically yew, bay laurel, and boxwood.

HEDGE TOPIARY

• Keep cutting tools sharp at all times.
• The simplest topiary design is one that is closest to the natural shape of the plant.
• Take time when clipping and shaping, especially in the formative stages. Stand back frequently to assess your progress.
• Work from the top downward and from the center outward, moving from side to side.
• Use the tips of the shears rather than the flat of the blades to cut curved surfaces.

◀ A BIRD IN THE HAND...
Imaginative shapes and figures, such as this bird, can make a hedge line interesting and eye-catching.

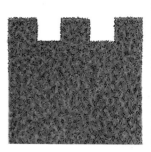

▶ CASTELLATION
Geometric shapes suit formal hedges, but they must be regularly maintained.

How to Grow a Pleached Hedge

A strong framework is needed to establish a pleached hedge. The main support posts for each tree's trunk must be driven at least 24in (60cm) into the ground and be as tall as the intended finished hedge. For the best effect, the spacing between the posts should be about 8ft (2.5m). Endposts will be needed a short distance from the first and last tree, so that the framework can support the entire extent of their growth. Horizontal battens or wires, for a less obtrusive effect, form the horizontal framework to which the lateral branches will be tied. Plant trees in late autumn, and prune away any shoots below the bottom wire or batten. Trim established pleached hedges as for shrubby hedge plants.

Cut back branches growing below the framework

Tie in lateral branches securely to the framework

Add extra ties to the leading shoot as it grows

Shorten long lateral branches back to a strong sideshoot

For uniformity, train all branches in the same direction

Train leading shoots to the top part of the framework

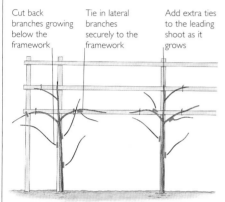

1 **Align as many** lateral branches as possible onto the framework on planting, and tie in the leading shoot. Remove any branches that cannot be readily secured to the framework, including those growing below it.

2 **Train the leading shoot** horizontally once it reaches the top of the framework. Pinch out all new shoots except for those that can be intertwined onto the framework so that all the spaces are filled in.

For the best formal effect, keep line of cuts perfectly straight

Weave together and tie in suitably placed shoots

Cut back wayward shoots to a sideways-facing bud

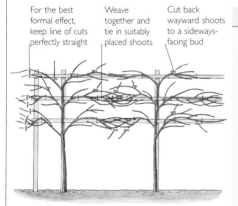

3 **Cut back all new** sideshoots that extend beyond the limits of the framework to a sideways-facing bud. As the gaps between the trees narrow, their sideshoots can be drawn and tied together.

PLANTS FOR PLEACHING

Start with three- or four-year-old trees with strong and straight leading shoots, with lateral branches at or near the height of the lowest horizontal support on the framework.
Carpinus betulus (**Hornbeam**) Deciduous trees with spring catkins, winged fruits and yellow foliage in autumn, and silvered bark in winter.
Fagus sylvatica (**Common beech**) Deciduous trees with a long, straight, smooth, silver-gray trunk. The fresh green leaves turn coppery in autumn, often persisting on clipped trees.
Platanus × hispanica (**London plane**) Deciduous, vigorous trees with flaking brown, grey and cream bark when mature, and bright green, 3–5 lobed leaves. Clusters of fruits persist into autumn and winter.
Tilia (**Linden**) Deciduous, usually long-lived trees grown for their colorful young shoots, broad foliage, and sweetly scented flowers.

RENOVATING A HEDGE

Quite commonly, gardeners are faced with an established hedge that has either been neglected or has grown too large. Where there are dead sections, a bare base, or a very severe weed infestation, the best option may be to remove it and start over, but this is hard work and expensive if contracted out. It is well worth attempting renovation even if removal is ultimately necessary.

WHAT TO CUT AND WHEN

Renovation work is likely to require pruners, loppers, a curved pruning saw, a long pruner, and sturdy gloves. Evergreen hedges are best dealt with in early spring, whereas deciduous hedges are best tackled in winter, when there will be less leafy waste and less disturbance of an active wildlife habitat. Both types of hedges are tackled in the same way.

The first task is to redefine with tall stakes the intended hedge line, which may have become lost to weed growth or gradual expansion of the hedge. Once the stakes are in place, remove growth that is clearly out of line together with dead and congested branches. Start at the base and work up to the top. To help the hedge recover from the renovation, apply a spring dressing of a general fertilizer and a deep mulch of well-rotted organic matter. Deciduous species will usually respond to the increased light levels, reduction of competition, and the stimulus of pruning by producing new shoots from the base in the following growing season.

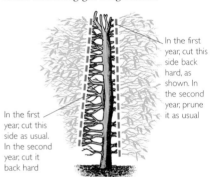

In the first year, cut this side back hard, as shown. In the second year, prune it as usual

In the first year, cut this side as usual. In the second year, cut it back hard

REDUCING THE WIDTH
Where the purpose of the operation is to reduce the width of a well-maintained hedge, it is advisable to deal with the two sides in successive years.

THINNING OLD STEMS
With loppers or a pruning saw, remove old, congested shoots from the base. Many plants will produce new growth in this region.

HOW TO USE A FRAME

As renovation work proceeds, careful attention must be paid to establishing the desirable narrow, sloping-sided profile of a hedge. Set up a template at the end of the hedge using a wooden frame and taut string. Define the height with more string running along both sides of the top of the hedge.

REDEFINING SHAPE
Cut an overgrown hedge using a post-and-string template to realign the shape (see inset).

Cutting Hedges Severely

Some plants will not tolerate severe cutting back into old wood. The renovation process should be planned for more than one season, therefore, gradually thinning out the established growth. Although most conifers will satisfactorily regrow in mild climates after hard pruning, it is a risky undertaking to cut into very old wood. Replacement rather than renovation is invariably the best option for conifers.

SEVERE CUTTING

Popular hedge plants that will respond to drastic pruning include:

Carpinus betulus (Hornbeam) Deciduous tree; renovate in autumn or early winter.

Corylus avellana (European hazel) Deciduous tree; renovate in late winter.

Crataegus monogyna (Singleseed hawthorn) Deciduous tree; renovate in winter.

Escallonia rubra Evergreen shrub; renovate in mid- to late spring.

Fagus sylvatica (Common beech) Deciduous tree; renovate in winter.

Ilex aquifolium (Common holly) Evergreen tree; reasonably tolerant of spring renovation.

Taxus baccata (English yew) Evergreen conifer; reasonably tolerant of spring renovation.

SECTION THROUGH CONIFER HEDGE
Regularly trimmed conifers have a dense, even surface, but are leafless within. Most will not produce new shoots from this old, bare wood.

Dealing with Splayed-out Growth

Hedges have a tight form, and this can be damaged by the effects of wind or snow. Remove heavy snow to avoid the risk of damage and splaying out of branches. Splayed-out growth can be tied in (*see below*), but if the branch is broken, either trim off the damaged part or remove the branch completely. To disguise the gap, reposition adjacent branches and tie them in using rubber tree ties or soft twine.

1 **Check the branch** for signs of damage. If the wood has been split, remove the branch with a pair of loppers or pruners. Otherwise, it can be tied back in.

2 **Tie the branch in** using soft material in case the tie is forgotten as the growth extends. Ideally, use soft garden twine, a rubber tree tie, or nylon tights or a stocking.

PROPAGATING YOUR OWN HEDGE

THE MAJORITY OF PLANTS suitable for hedges can be propagated at home, and this is a feasible option if a hedge is planned well in advance. For most garden situations, however, hedges need to be quickly established, and an important step toward this is to start with plants at least one year old. Unless you need to keep costs down, therefore, or you have a personal interest in raising your own plants, it is usual to start a hedge with well-grown plants supplied by a local garden center, nursery, or by mail order.

PROPAGATION FROM HARDWOOD CUTTINGS

Several species of deciduous hedge plants may be propagated from dormant hardwood cuttings. It is one of the easiest and least costly forms of propagation, and it requires no special skill, other than knowing which plants are suitable (*see box, below*). In early autumn, prepare the ground for the cuttings while it is still warm (*see p.37*), and take the cuttings immediately after leaf fall or just before bud break. Look for healthy, vigorous, fully mature shoots, avoiding weak or very spindly growth. Section these into lengths and insert into the precultivated outdoor bed, preferably one with open, friable soil. If the rooted plants are large enough by the following autumn, transplant them to their final positions. It is possible to insert hardwood cuttings direct into the final planting site, but for them to be successful, the hedge line must be kept free of weeds and well mulched.

1 **Push your spade** vertically into the soil and press it forward slightly to form a flat-backed trench about 7in (18cm) deep.

2 **Take strong** straight stems with healthy buds. Remove any leaves and trim cuttings to 9–12in (23–30cm) long. Cut just above and below a bud.

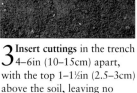

3 **Insert cuttings** in the trench 4–6in (10–15cm) apart, with the top 1–1½in (2.5–3cm) above the soil, leaving no more than 3 buds exposed.

4 **Firm in the soil** around the cuttings, rake the surface, and label. Space any additional rows 12–15in (30–38cm) apart.

HARDWOOD CUTTINGS

Atriplex	Olearia (Daisy bush)
Aucuba	Philadelphus (Mock orange)
Chaenomeles (Japonica)	Potentilla
Cornus (Dogwood)	Ribes (Flowering currant)
Elaeagnus (Oleaster)	Rosa (Rose)
Forsythia	Salix (Willow)
Hibiscus	Sambucus (Elder)
Leycesteria	Tamarix (Tamarisk)
Ligustrum (Privet)	Weigela

SOFTWOOD AND SEMIRIPE CUTTINGS

Almost all species of suitable hedge plants can be propagated from soft green shoot tips removed from spring to late summer. Firm cuttings taken from semiripe wood in late summer are more likely to succeed.

Choose cutting material from shoots that are typical, healthy, and strong, and make sure that their handling time is minimal. To prepare the cuttings, trim them into 2½–4in (6–10cm) lengths. If the cutting has large foliage, like that of a hydrangea, reduce the leaves in size by cutting them in half cleanly with a sharp knife; this reduces moisture loss and it allows better housing of the cuttings in their rooting container. Sometimes, success is improved where short sideshoots are pulled off with a portion of the main stem still attached to the base of the shoot. These are called heel cuttings, and the "tail" of the main stem heel must be trimmed back carefully.

Finally, insert the cuttings into a rooting medium, which is usually a well-drained soil mix (*see below*), although horticultural rock wool can be a good alternative for plants that are difficult to root.

Discard tip

Cut leaflets in half

Angled cut above leaf joint

Fungicide

Dip stem in hormone rooting powder

1 **Remove a healthy shoot of** the current season's growth (here a softwood cutting from a rose). Place the cuttings in a plastic bag to keep them fresh.

2 **Cut the shoot** into sections so that each section retains one leaf at the top. Discard the tip and trim the leaflets to reduce moisture loss.

3 **Dip the cuttings** in rooting powder and fungicide, then insert them into horticultural rock wool, as shown here, or a cuttings soil mix.

HOW TO ROOT SOFTWOOD AND SEMIRIPE CUTTINGS

Mix an equal quantity of peat or coir with coarse sand or vermiculite to make a suitable cuttings soil mix. Dip the ends of the cuttings into a rooting powder – one with added fungicide replaces the need for a separate dip – and insert the cuttings firmly and at well-spaced intervals into the soil mix. Use a propagating case or 3–4in (8–10cm) pots that can be covered with clear plastic. Water the soil mix well, and place the cuttings in cool shade. Inspect them regularly to remove any dead leaves and to ensure a humid environment by keeping the soil mix moist but not saturated. Rooting time varies from weeks to months. Watch for new growth; a gentle tug on a cutting will give some idea of the rooting stage.

SOME PLANTS TO TRY

Abelia × *grandiflora*
Camellia japonica
Ceanothus thyrsiflorus (Blue blossom)
Cotoneaster lacteus
Hydrangea macrophylla
Lavandula angustifolia (English lavender)
Lonicera nitida (Shrubby honeysuckle)
Potentilla fruticosa
Rosmarinus officinalis (Rosemary)
Spiraea 'Arguta'
Symphoricarpos albus (Snowberry)
Viburnum tinus (Laurustinus)

HEDGE PROBLEMS

CAREFULLY CHOSEN, WELL-MAINTAINED PLANTS in a suitable location with good soil preparation are the least likely to succumb to pests, diseases, and disorders. If, however, an individual plant in a hedge line is damaged or lost, it will cause permanent, partial disfigurement, and the hedge may lose some or all of its effectiveness. Planning and good management are therefore essential if a hedge is to remain trouble free.

PESTS AND DISEASES

As a rule, well-grown hedge plants are least likely to suffer significant insect damage; use of insecticide is justified only in the case of serious attacks. A few common ones to look out for include aphids, which can cause young shoots to become curled and severely distorted; caterpillars, which eat holes into leaves; and red spider mites, which cause a fine yellow mottling of leaf surfaces, and where the pest really takes hold there may be defoliation. Leaf miners, scale insects, and thrips can be the cause of various leaf or shoot damage.

Like insects, many diseases are specific to certain plants, but there are some that affect a wide range, such as phytophthora and honey fungus. Fireblight can attack hawthorns, cotoneasters, and a few other relatives causing leaves to shrivel and die. Powdery mildews result in white fungal growth mostly on the upper surface of leaves, which turn yellow and fall early.

On some garden sites, hedges are vulnerable to damage from deer or rabbits. This can be devastating, especially during establishment; erect protective fencing or install individual plant guards around hedge lines on afffected sites.

BEECH APHID

POWDERY MILDEW

PESTS
Beech aphids are a frequent pest of beech hedges. They occur as a dense, woolly mass on the under surface of leaves. From here, an excretion of sticky honeydew can be a nuisance when it drips onto surrounding plants.

PHYTOPHTHORA

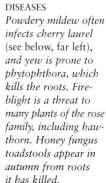

DISEASES
Powdery mildew often infects cherry laurel (see below, far left), and yew is prone to phytophthora, which kills the roots. Fireblight is a threat to many plants of the rose family, including hawthorn. Honey fungus toadstools appear in autumn from roots it has killed.

FIREBLIGHT

HONEY FUNGUS

CULTURAL PROBLEMS

It is often impossible to fully restore a damaged, established hedge, although such problems are frequently cultural, so they can be avoided. For example, hedges that are not regularly maintained may become top heavy and fall apart, and where clipping is resumed after neglect, cutting into old wood can leave bare patches. Conifers, especially, have a natural tendency to become bare at the base.

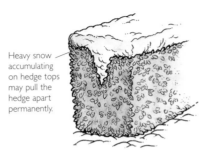

Heavy snow accumulating on hedge tops may pull the hedge apart permanently.

Very low temperatures can cause shoot damage to frost-tender species – usually in the form of wilted growth tips and blackened foliage. Drought typically results in curled or desiccated leaves in deciduous plants; in conifers the foliage may die from the base upwards. To reduce the risk, add organic matter to drought-susceptible soils at the preparation stage, and always mulch after planting. Water establishing hedges sufficiently to avoid any check to growth.

SNOW DAMAGE
Heavy falls of snow on a flat-topped hedge can cause shoot breakage. Always clear snow from such hedges as soon as possible.

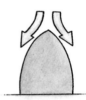

POINTED HEDGE
A hedge with a pointed or rounded top discourages the accumulation of snow. The shape must be produced during training.

DEALING WITH DEAD PATCHES

Dead patches can arise as a symptom of progressive disease, such as phytophthora or fireblight, and may eventually require hedge replacement. However, unsightly patches are often the result of physical damage caused by careless trimming, shoot breakage following heavy snowfall, frost damage, or wind scorch, and the bases of coniferous hedges are naturally prone to dying out. Many of these situations can be improved by thoughtful trimming and training, and patient tying in. Before you decide to replant a hedge, it is always worth an attempt to try and restore its visual attractiveness first.

1 **Assess area** of dead or scorched foliage. Check that it is confined to branch extremities; if not, there may be an underlying problem.

2 **Remove completely** all affected shoots. Unless damage is minimal, this will leave an unsightly hole, especially in a formal hedge.

3 **Tie stake** securely to a main branch, then tie nearby branches onto it. New growth will soon disguise the stake and the hole.

RECOMMENDED HEDGES

CHOICE OF HEDGING is a matter of both suitability and personal preference. This is a long-lasting investment, so plan carefully and become familiar with the plants. The range of trees and shrubs available is very wide, and most could be planted in a line to form a hedge; this catalog is a guide to those plants that are known to make successful hedges under most conditions. There is a brief description of each plant and its suitability, together with a summary of the recommended pruning. Some of the plants here are widely used as formal hedges; others are less often used but have potential as informal hedges.

☒ *Prefers full sun* ☒ *Prefers light or dappled shade* ☒ *Prefers partial shade* ☀ *Tolerates full shade* ❀ *Dislikes transplanting* ᵖᴴ *Needs acid soil* ◊ *Prefers well-drained soil* ◔ *Prefers moist soil* ● *Prefers wet soil* Hardiness zone ranges are given as Zx-x **Min. °F/°C** *Indicates minimum temperature for tender plants.*

A

Abelia × grandiflora
Vigorous evergreen or semi-evergreen to 10ft (3m) tall with arching branches of dark green leaves 2in (5cm) long. Bears fragrant, pink-tinged white flowers ¾in (2cm) long from summer to autumn. 'Francis Mason' is a fine cultivar, less vigorous, with darker green leaves that are edged with yellow. Grow in fertile soil in full sun, with shelter from cold, dry winds; may be susceptible to damage in areas prone to severe cold. Prune after flowering.
  Abelia schumannii is a hardier, deciduous species, which can also be grown as

ABELIA × GRANDIFLORA

an informal hedge in a situation where winter cover is not required. It bears rose-pink flowers that are marked with orange.
☒◊ **Z6–9**

Alnus glutinosa
(Common alder)
The alder is naturally a large, broad, conical tree with oval, dark green leaves 4in (10cm) long and brown male catkins 4in (10cm) long in winter and early spring. Female catkins, borne on the same plant, are broader, shorter, and develop into ovoid, small, woody fruits in summer. Alder is hardy and can be contained by trimming in the autumn. It tolerates a wide range of soil conditions, including wet sites. There are interesting selections, such as 'Aurea', with golden shoots and young leaves, or 'Laciniata', with finely cut foliage, which are also worth considering.
☒◊ **Z3–7**

◀ DISTINCT DEFINITION *Hedges of varying heights and styles delineate separate areas of a garden.*

Amelanchier lamarckii
(Shadbush, Snowy mespilus)
A graceful, potentially large
plant, which needs space as
a hedge; it can grow in
excess of 20ft (6m). The
leaves, 3in (8cm) long, are
bronze when young, changing
to dark green and then
developing striking orange
and red tints in autumn. In
spring there is a fine display
of white flowers, which are
borne in pendent clusters
2½–5in (6–12 cm) long. They
are followed by small, purple
fruits. ▣ Ꝑ ◊ Z5–9

Amelanchier canadensis
(Shadbush) is a more dense
and contained plant, bearing
erect clusters of white flowers,
and with more yellow to the
autumn color. Its suckering
habit can be a disadvantage,
but provides a ready means of
propagation. Prune to reduce
density of shoots in winter.
▣ Ꝑ ◊ Z3–7

Arbutus unedo
(Strawberry tree)
Spreading, woody, evergreen
shrub with distinctive peeling,
red-brown bark when mature.

ARBUTUS UNEDO

It will eventually reach up
to 20ft (6m) in favorable
conditions, but it is amenable
to containment. The oval,
light green leaves are 4in
(10cm) long and slightly
toothed. Pink-tinged, white
flowers resembling those of
lily-of-the-valley are borne in
pendent clusters in autumn,
and these are followed by
spherical, rough, red fruits ¾in
(2cm) in diameter, which are
edible but flavorless. The
strawberry tree does best
growing in a nonalkaline soil
in sun, although it will
tolerate lime, and it is a good
choice in windy, coastal sites.
Only minimal pruning is
needed to contain the hedge;
this is best carried out in
spring. An interesting choice
for a hedge, although it is a
considerable investment.
▣ ◊ Z7–9

Atriplex halimus
(Tree purslane)
A bushy, semi-evergreen,
shrub up to 6ft (2m) tall with
leathery, gray leaves 2½in
(6cm) long, which tolerates
dry, windy situations and is a
good choice for coastal areas.

Inconspicuous white flowers
are produced in spring.
Damaged shoots should be
lightly trimmed in early
spring.
▣ ◊ Z7–9

Aucuba japonica
(Japanese laurel)
The natural, untrained habit
of aucubas is to grow into a
rounded shrub up to 13ft
(4m) high. The leaves are
thick, oval, pointed, deep
green, glossy, and 4–10in
(10–25cm) long. Small, star-
shaped, maroon flowers are
produced in spring. The
species has plain green leaves,
but the many variegated
cultivars are widely planted
and familiar: 'Crotonifolia'
and 'Gold Dust' have leaves
spotted with yellow and bear
female flowers, producing
bright red berries from late
summer to early spring where
a male cultivar, such as
'Crassifolia', is included in the
planting. These reliable shrubs
grow well on most soils and
will tolerate both shade and
dry soil. Prune shoots to
shape in spring. Aucubas

AMELANCHIER LAMARCKII

AUCUBA JAPONICA

make imposing hedges, and they will grow quite quickly once they are established. They provide both color and structure throughout the year in formal situations, and make effective and striking border hedges in country or town gardens.
◨–◪◊–◊ Z6–10

B

Baccharis halimifolia
(Groundsel bush,
Sea myrtle)
A fast-growing, deciduous shrub up to 10ft (3m) high and bearing coarsely toothed, gray-green leaves 1–3in (3–8cm) long. Large clusters of white, groundsel-like flowers are produced from late summer into autumn, and are followed female plants by masses of silver-white, downy, thistlelike seedheads. It is very tolerant of dry soils and seaside exposure and amenable to training as a hedge, for which it is best cut in the spring.
◨◊ Z3–7

Bupleurum fruticosum
(Shrubby hare's ear)
A dense, slender-branched evergreen growing to 6ft (2m) high and bearing tough, dull sea-green leaves 3in (8cm) long, which have gray undersides. The compound umbels of small, star-shaped, yellow flowers appear in summer. A suitable shrub for well-drained, sunny sites, it will make a satisfactory hedge in coastal gardens, where it shows a good tolerance of hard pruning.
◨◊ Z7–10

BERBERIS (BARBERRY)

A large genus of spiny, evergreen and deciduous species, with attractive flowers, usually in spring, colored leaves, often providing autumn interest, and colored fruits. These features and their tolerance of trimming make many excellent hedge plants. They succeed on any well-drained soil in sunny or shady situations. Berberis species make good formal hedges, but are equally suitable for informal hedges, and there are also dwarf species.
Z5–9.

Evergreen
Berberis × *stenophylla* grows to 10ft (3m) with narrow, spiny, dark green leaves and deep yellow flowers followed by purple-black fruits. The dwarf 'Corallina Compacta' can be used as edging: other forms have red or orange flowers and colored leaves. Other good evergreens are the

BERBERIS THUNBERGII
'DART'S RED LADY'

large *B. julianae* and the smaller *B. verruculosa*.
B. darwinii (p.27) is upright and vigorous, to 10ft (3m), bearing profuse, dark orange flowers with a second flush in autumn. Trim in summer after flowering; can be hard pruned for containment.

Deciduous or semi-evergreen
B. thunbergii grows to 8ft (2.5m), with dramatic red autumn color. Cultivars include the dwarf, red-purple-leaved 'Bagatelle' and the yellow-leaved 'Aurea'. Hard cutting improves spring leaf color. Other good choices are the large *B.* × *ottawensis*, especially 'Superba', its red stems and purple-green leaves best hard pruned, and *B. buxifolia*, also large, but the dwarf cultivar 'Pygamaea' is suitable for edging. The gray-green *B. wilsoniae* turns a good red in autumn.

BERBERIS DARWINII

BRACHYGLOTTIS 'SUNSHINE'

BUXUS SEMPERVIRENS

Camellia

Camellia japonica is a widely grown evergreen shrub with large, strong, glossy leaves 2–4in (5–10cm) long. There are many cultivars with various flower forms and colors, blooming from late winter to early spring. 'Alba Plena' is an excellent white.

Other camellias are also good: although cultivars of *C. reticulata* and *C. sasanqua* are only suitable for the mildest of climates, the many *C. × williamsii* cultivars, mostly in shades of pink, including the semi-double 'Donation' and the single 'J.C. Williams', in general flower better than *C. japonica* in areas with cooler summers. The flowers also drop neatly as they fade.

Camellias require very little trimming, and it is best done immediately after flowering. They will do best in moist, acid soil and in partial shade: keep them out of early morning sun, which can damage the flower buds after a frosty night.

◼ pH ◊ Z6–8

Brachyglottis 'Sunshine'

A hardy, well-tried, low-growing shrub up to about 3ft (1m) high, with white hairy leaves, dark green above, which are robust in exposed situations. Produces an abundance of bright-yellow daisy flowers. Can be grown to good effect as an informal hedge but is also tolerant of hard pruning and shaping in the spring. A suitable choice for hedging in seaside gardens.

◼◊ Z9–10

Buxus sempervirens

(Boxwood)

Naturally a large shrub up to 15ft (5m) high, boxwood is very amenable to containment and clipping, and well proven as a candidate for hedges, edging, and topiary *(p.10)*. The glossy, dark green leaves are up to 1¼ in (3cm) long. There are numerous selections worth considering, including the compact 'Suffruticosa', which is particularly good for formal edging, and variegated forms including 'Latifolia Maculata' and 'Marginata'.

Other boxwood species are also successful hedging plants; *B. microphylla*, a slow-growing plant, does best in partial shade and is particularly useful for smaller hedges. Trim boxwood at least once a year, in late spring, and encourage growth with a fertilizer dressing and surface mulch.

◼◊ Z6–9

C

Callistemon

(Bottlebrush)

Fine shrubs in warm climates, bottlebrushes are interesting evergreens, so-called because of their bottlebrush-like spikes of colorful flowers, but are only reliable in milder areas, where they require full sun. The growth habit is spreading, and a hedge line should have minimal pruning. The lance-shaped leaves of *C. citrinus* release a lemon scent when crushed, and the cultivar 'Splendens' produces spikes of beautiful crimson flowers.

◼◊–◊ Z10–11

CAMELLIA JAPONICA
'RUBESCENS MAJOR'

CARAGANA ARBORESCENS 'NANA'

Caragana arborescens
(Peashrub)
A hardy, erect, spiny shrub with compound, light green leaves to 3in (8cm) long, composed of up to 12 leaflets. Pealike, yellow flowers are produced in early summer. An extremely tough plant that will do well on all types of soils, even dry ones, and in exposed sites; it is successfully used as a hedging plant in quite harsh climates. Requires very little pruning.
☒◊–◊ Z2–8

Carpinus betulus
(Hornbeam)
An excellent, hardy hedging subject *(pp.19, 21, 32)*, generally similar in trained habit to beech (*Fagus, p.63*) but distinguished by its rougher textured, saw-toothed leaves and its characteristic bracted fruits. The mid-green, oval, pointed, toothed leaves are 3–5in (7–12cm) long and heavily ribbed. They are borne on slender branchlets and turn first a good yellow and then brown in autumn. Clusters of inconspicuous,

catkinlike flowers appear in spring, contained in leafy bracts that persist as an attractive feature. Hornbeam is easily grown as a hedge and does especially well on chalky soils. If it is trimmed in late summer, a large proportion of the crisp, dead leaves are retained well into winter. Established hedges tolerate hard pruning (**Z4–8**). *Carpinus caroliniana*, American hornbeam, is a smaller species that is also successfully used as hedging.
☒–☒◊ Z3–9

Ceanothus
(Californian lilac)
Ceanothus thyrsiflorus, blue blossom *(p.26)*, is a vigorous, evergreen shrub with arching branches of toothed, glossy leaves 1¼–3in (3–8cm) long, and bearing dense clusters of pale blue flowers along the branches in early summer. Prune after flowering for containment and to ensure productive flowering shoots. Suitable only in warm climates, they often tolerate poor growing conditions.

CEANOTHUS 'CONCHA'

CHAENOMELES SPECIOSA 'MOERLOOSII'

There are also good hybrid cultivars such as 'Autumnal Blue', 'Burkwoodii', and 'Dark Star'. Ceanothus hedges will reach 10ft (3m) high and need plenty of space. All prefer a sunny location.
☒◊ Z8–10

Chaenomeles speciosa
(Flowering quince)
A thorny hedge plant, seen to best effect where informally grown but amenable to formal clipping. Oval, glossy leaves 1½–3½ in (4–9cm) long accompany spring clusters of scarlet or crimson flowers *(p.27)*. On favorable sites large, yellow, aromatic fruits resembling quinces are produced in autumn. There are many cultivars, including the white-flowered 'Nivalis' and the pink-flowered 'Moerloosei'. *Chaenomeles japonica*, Japonica or Japanese quince, has smaller leaves and orange to red flowers. Good subjects for protective barriers, up to 8ft (2.5m) high. Prune in late spring to encourage spurs.
☒–☒◊ Z5–9

CHAMAECYPARIS LAWSONIANA
'PEMBURY BLUE'

Chamaecyparis lawsoniana
(Lawson false cypress)
Naturally a very tall, hardy, coniferous tree, but suitable for trimming into a formal hedge. Bears dense fans of aromatic, scalelike leaves. Grows well on moist acid to neutral soils. There are many cultivars, including foliage color forms from the silvery blue 'Pembury Blue' to the gold 'Stardust'. Other species are also suitable as hedges, including C. *pisifera*, the Sawara cypress, which bears mossy green leaves, silvery beneath. Numerous cultivars are available and can be used for hedging, including the blue-green 'Boulevard' and golden yellow 'Filifera Aurea'. All are susceptible to phytophthora root rot. Trim closely from spring to autumn; do not cut into older wood, as it will not resprout.
▣ 凵 ◊ Z5–9

Choisya ternata
(Mexican orange blossom)
A compact, evergreen plant up to 8ft (2.5m) high, bearing dark green, aromatic leaves in groups of three, with leaflets 1½–3in (4–8cm) long. Fragrant, white flowers are borne in late spring, usually with a second flush late in the season. Does well in a wide range of situations. Requires minimal pruning.
▣ ◊ Z9–10

Cornus stolonifera
(Red osier dogwood)
A vigorous, deciduous shrub growing up to 6ft (2m) tall, and a member of the fine garden plant genus *Cornus*, which contains many excellent and interesting trees and shrubs. *Cornus stolonifera* makes a striking feature hedge, providing excellent winter interest in the form of attractive, dark red stems; these are produced after stooling or other hard pruning in the spring. 'Flaviramea' (p.33) is a yellow-stemmed cultivar. C. *alba* is another red-stemmed species, which grows a little taller and also contains a number of suitable cultivars, some with variegated foliage.
▣ ◊ –◊ Z2–8

CHOISYA TERNATA

CORNUS STOLONIFERA
'FLAVIRAMEA'

Corylus avellana
(European hazel)
The hazel is naturally a hardy, multistemmed shrub that reaches 15ft (5m) if uncut, but it is amenable to trimming as a contained hedge. The green leaves are round-tipped and toothed and provide an attractive yellow color in autumn. Another decorative feature is the pendent, yellow male catkins of early spring. The female flowers, which are borne on the same plants, are tiny and red.

Hazel makes a strong, well-furnished hedge, very suitable as a boundary. *Corylus avellana* has several interesting cultivars, such as 'Heterophylla', which has deeply lobed leaves, and 'Aurea', a yellow-leaved form. C. *maxima*, the filbert, has larger leaves than C. *avellana* and also produces edible nuts. The selection C. *maxima* 'Purpurea' is also a good choice as an informal hedge plant. All these hazels should be lightly trimmed to a formal shape.
▣ –▨ ◊ Z3–9

Cotoneaster

There are many cotoneasters, evergreen and deciduous, varying from trees to ground-cover plants. *Cotoneaster lacteus* (**Z7–9**) is an excellent dense, evergreen hedging subject, growing naturally to 12ft (4m). The dark green, tough leaves are prominently veined and 1½–3½in (3.5–9cm) long, with white felt on the undersides. White flowers are followed by large clusters of brick-red berries, which persist into the winter. Benefits from light trimming to maintain a formal shape.

Also worth considering are *C. franchetii*, semi-evergreen with white, pink-flushed flowers and scarlet berries, *C. frigidus* 'Cornubia', which is semi-evergreen and bears abundant fruits, and *C. divaricatus* (**Z5–7**), deciduous with pink flowers and good autumn color.
◙–◙◊ **Zones vary**

Crataegus monogyna
(Singleseed hawthorn)
An excellent, cost-effective hedge plant that thrives under all but the wettest soil and

CRATAEGUS LAEVIGATA 'PAUL'S SCARLET'

site conditions. Its deterrent thorns make it an excellent choice as a protective barrier, and it withstands severe wind. The glossy leaves are 2in (5cm) long and attractive for their 3- to 7-lobed form. The white flowers are spectacular in late spring and are followed by glossy, dark red fruits. Formal trimming is best after flowering, or may be done in the autumn. Other species of hawthorn also worth considering include *C. laevigata* and its cultivars, including the double pink 'Rosea Flore Pleno' and the dramatically colored double 'Paul's Scarlet'. The fruits of *C. crus-galli*, the cockspur thorn, persist into winter, as do those of *C. phaenopyrum*, the Washington hawthorn, which also turns a good orange color in autumn.
◙–◙◊–◊ **Z4–8**

× Cupressocyparis leylandii
(Leyland cypress)
A very vigorous, evergreen conifer (*p.11*), which will grow relatively quickly to a great height if left untrimmed;

this accounts for its original recommendation as a fast-established hedge or screen. It is an excellent, dense hedge plant, tolerant of a wide range of soils and situations, but one that must not be considered unless you are willing and able to undertake regular trimming. Ideally a Leyland hedge should be cut three times each year, and where it is kept under careful control by continual clipping it forms an attractive and effective hedge. Overgrown Leyland cypress hedges are well documented as a source of strife between adjoining property owners, because of the rapid growth, which can obscure both light and views. Branch and root encroach-ment can also cause problems. The cultivar 'Castlewellan' is somewhat slower growing, but still not a suitable choice for small gardens. Leyland cypress hedges will take a great deal of moisture and nutrients from the soil, and there needs to be space between the hedge line and cultivated ground.
◙–◙◊ **Z6–9**

COTONEASTER LACTEUS

× *CUPRESSOCYPARIS LEYLANDII*

CUPRESSUS MACROCARPA
'GOLDCREST'

Cupressus macrocarpa
(Monterey cypress)
A well-tried coniferous plant
amenable to trimming to a
formal shape and useful for
coastal gardens. It is fast
growing, and the lemon-
scented foliage is best
trimmed in late summer. Very
young plants are susceptible
to frost, and on some sites
it can be prone to losing
individual plants. The cultivar
'Goldcrest' produces yellow
foliage, at its best in full sun.
Cupressus sempervirens, the
Italian cypress, is also used
for hedging, and requires
broadly the same conditions
and treatment.
◙◊ **Z7–10**

Cytisus scoparius
(Scotch broom)
A hardy shrub to 6ft (2m)
tall. Deciduous, but its green,
whippy stems give it an
evergreen appearance. In late
spring it bears an abundance
of bright yellow, pealike
flowers. *Cytisus scoparius*
f. *andreanus* has yellow
flowers blotched with red,
and the cultivar 'Cornish

Cream' has creamy white
flowers. The brooms are
hardy and thrive on most
soils, provided they are well
drained. They can produce an
attractive informal hedge line,
but are not suitable for
exposure to strong winds.
Pruning should be kept to a
minimum, shortening older
stems after flowering.
◙☀◊ **Z6–8**

D

Deutzia scabra
(Fuzzy deutzia)
An easily grown, upright,
flowering hedge plant up to
10ft (3m) in height. The dark
green, deciduous leaves are
3in (8cm) long, and dense,
upright clusters of white or
pink-tinged, honey-scented
flowers are produced in
summer. Mature shoots have
attractive peeling bark.
'Candidissima' is taller, with
double, white flowers.
Deutzia gracilis may be used
as a hedge to 3ft (1m) high.
Prune to thin out older shoots
immediately after flowering.
◙◊ **Z6–8**

DEUTZIA SCABRA

ELEAGNUS × EBBINGEI

E

Elaeagnus
(Oleaster)
Tough, fast-growing shrubs,
including several evergreens
that make good candidates
for hedging. *Elaeagnus
macrophylla* (**Z7–9**) is a
strong evergreen that
responds well to formal
training by trimming in late
summer. The glossy leaves are
4in (10cm) long, and silver-
scaly beneath. Small, fragrant,
cream flowers are produced in
autumn. Tolerant of partial
shade, dry soil, and seaside
exposure.
   The faster-growing
E. × ebbingei is also a good
choice. It has numerous
variegated forms, including
'Gilt Edge' (*p.32*) with golden
leaf margins. Another species
is *E. pungens*, which also has
good variegated forms;
'Maculata' has gold leaf
centers. *E. angustifolia*
(**Z3–8**), a spiny shrub with
willowlike, silvery leaves, may
also be used.
◙–◙◊ **Zones vary**

ESCALLONIA RUBRA
'WOODSIDE'

Escallonia rubra

Vigorous evergreen (*p.26*) with dark green, often sticky leaves up to 3in (8cm) long. Loose clusters of small, tubular, crimson flowers are borne through summer and into autumn. A good, fast-growing, dense hedging plant that does well in gardens near the sea and is reasonably hardy inland; one drawback is that it can rob surrounding soil of moisture and nutrients. The cultivar 'Crimson Spire' makes an excellent hedge plant and bears deep crimson flowers. 'Woodside' is a little less vigorous, to about 5ft (1.5m) but has a tendency to revert to *E. rubra*. Other escallonias are good hedging plants, including the white-flowered 'Iveyi', 'Apple Blossom', and the Donard range. All escallonias respond well to regular clipping.
◙◊ Z8–9

Euonymus japonicus

(Japanese spindle tree)
A dense, bushy evergreen with bluntly and finely toothed, thick, glossy, dark green leaves to 2½in (6cm) long. A good hedging plant in sun or shade, doing best on moist soils. In dry, sheltered sites it may be prone to powdery mildew. Numerous cultivars are available including 'Albomarginatus' with white leaf margins, 'Aureus' with a central gold marking, and the shorter 'Ovatus Aureus' with golden yellow leaf margins. The variegated leaf forms are most effective when grown in full sun. Trim shoots lightly after flowering.

Euonymus fortunei cultivars (Wintercreeper) are mound-forming types, which can be trained as low formal edging. It has a number of fine cultivars, including 'Emerald 'n' Gold', which has bright green leaves with yellow margins that become tinged with pink.

E. alatus (Burning bush) is a deciduous species of this diverse genus, and makes an interesting informal hedge, growing to 6ft (2m). It is notable for its striking red autumn leaf color. The fruits of all euonymus are mildly toxic if eaten. ◙–◙◊ Z4–9

FAGUS SYLVATICA

FORSYTHIA × INTERMEDIA

F

Fagus sylvatica

(Common beech)
A fine hedging plant, and usually relatively inexpensive. The leaves are up to 4in (10cm) long, at first silky-haired and pale green, becoming dark green and glossy, then golden yellow in autumn. Like hornbeam (*Carpinus, p.59*), with which beech is sometimes confused, hedges of beech will retain their attractive, brown, desiccated leaves into winter if trimming is done in late summer. Beech hedges are sometimes troubled by aphids. ◙–◙◊ Z5–7

Forsythia × intermedia

Bushy, vigorous, deciduous plant with finely toothed leaves to 4in (10cm) long. Makes a good internal hedge of a fairly loose form, up to 5ft (1.5m) high, with striking, bright yellow flowers in early spring. 'Lynwood' (*p.11*) is a good cultivar. Prune hard after flowering.
◙–◙◊ Z6–9

FUCHSIA MAGELLANICA

GARRYA ELLIPTICA

GRISELINA LITTORALIS 'DIXON'S CREAM'

Fuchsia magellanica

An upright plant with soft leaves ½–2½in (1.5–6 cm) long. In summer it bears a profusion of the small, pendulous flowers that are typical of fuchsias with red, pink, and purple parts.

A graceful hedge, growing up to 10ft (3m), this is at its best in mild frost-free climate areas. The hybrid 'Riccartonii' is also often used for hedging. Prune hard in spring.

☑–⬛◊–◊ Z6–9

Garrya elliptica
(Silk-tassel bush)

A dense, evergreen shrub (*p.29*) with gray-green leaves 3in (8cm) long, glossy or matte. It is prized for the gray catkins borne on male plants, which may be up to 8in (20cm) long and hang in clusters through winter until spring. The cultivar 'James Roof' is noted for having the longest catkins. This should be treated as a semiformal hedge, being lightly pruned with pruners in spring to contain it in an orderly shape while retaining potential catkin-bearing shoots. Plant as an internal hedge away from exposure, against a wall, or as a windbreak.

☑–⬛◊ Z8–10

Grevillea rosmariniifolia

An evergreen shrub up to 6ft (2m) high with narrow, linear leaves. In spring and summer bears clusters of small, red, tubular flowers, curled in bud. One of the hardier species of a fairly tender genus, suitable as an informal hedge in very mild areas. Prune growing tips to make plants bushier, and reduce shoots in number after flowering to contain size.

☑ ⵑ◊ Z9–10

Griselinia littoralis

A dense, attractive evergreen with glossy, apple green, leathery leaves up to 4in (10cm) long. Responds well to trimming to shape and thrives in coastal gardens, where it can be recommended as one of the quickest hedges to establish. It is hardier than *G. lucida*, sometimes found as a hedge in mild climate areas. 'Bantry Bay' and 'Dixon's Cream' are attractive variegated forms but generally do less well as hedge plants. Although tolerant of clipping into a formal hedge it is better trimmed to shape with pruners in spring; responds well to occasional careful hard cutting to reduce spread.

☑◊ Z8–9

H

Hamamelis mollis
(Chinese witch hazel)

A deciduous, erect shrub with mid-green leaves turning yellow in autumn. Makes an interesting trimmed hedge if clipped or pruned in spring immediately after the flowers fade. The fragrant, spidery, golden yellow flowers are the special feature, providing interest from mid- to late winter. Attractive cultivars are 'Goldcrest', a larger shrub, and the hybrid 'Brevipetala', which has orange or red features to its flowers.

HEBE RAKAIENSIS

Hamamelis × intermedia is an alternative, generally earlier-flowering than *H. mollis*; 'Diane' and 'Jelena' have red and coppery flowers.
⊡ – ▨ pH ◊ Z5–9

Hebe salicifolia

An evergreen shrub suitable for a divider hedge up to 6ft (1.8m) high. The narrow, pointed, green leaves are 5in (12cm) or more in length. Long, slender, pendent spires of white or pale blue flowers are produced in summer. *Hebe* 'Autumn Glory' is smaller, suited to low hedging up to 24in (60cm) high, and bears small, dark purple flowers from summer into autumn. There are many hebe species and cultivars, with flowers of white, red, and blue, and there are variegated forms. *Hebe albicans* is a rounded, tidy shrub with white flowers, up to 2ft (60cm) tall and suitable for low hedging, as is the similarly white-flowered *H. brachysiphon*. *H. rakaiensis* is a taller plant, up to 3ft (1m), with abundant large, white flowers in midsummer, which makes it a fine choice for a low hedge plant. All hebes do best on moist soil and full sun; all are evergreen and well worth considering as hedge plants subject to their individual hardiness; large-leaved types are usually more tender. Most hebes break well from older wood, which is helpful in containing their growth, but they are easily propagated and best replaced periodically. Prune lightly either in spring or after flowering.
⊡ – ▨ ◊ Z8–10

Hibiscus syriacus

Deciduous, upright shrub, to 10ft (3m), with 3-lobed, coarsely toothed leaves (Z5–9). Solitary or paired red, white, or blue trumpet flowers with prominent stamens are borne from summer to autumn. One of the hardier hibiscus, along with *H. sinosyriacus*. Large-flowered cultivars are 'Diana' with white flowers, PINK GIANT ('Flogi') with red-eyed, pink flowers and

HIBISCUS ROSA-SINENSIS 'SCARLET GIANT'

HIPPOPHAE RHAMNOIDES

'Woodbridge' with pink flowers. *Hibiscus rosa-sinensis* (**min 50°F/10°C**), with glossy, dark, evergreen leaves up to 6in (15cm) long, is suitable only in mild areas. There are many cultivars. A hedge of hibiscus is a relatively expensive feature, making it a choice for a short run in a sunny location. Hedges should be pruned minimally in late spring.
⊡ ◊ Zones vary

Hippophae rhamnoides

(Sea buckthorn)
Bushy shrub with spiny shoots and silver, scaly leaves 2½ in (6cm) long. Produces tiny yellow-green flowers in spring, with male and female flowers on separate plants: if both are grown, female plants bear small, bright orange berries in autumn, which remain on the bush in winter. Very tolerant of salt-laden winds and suitable for the outer borders of coastal gardens; also succeeds inland. Trim lightly in late summer to maintain a formal shape.
⊡ ◊ Z3–8

HYDRANGEA MACROPHYLLA '*GÉNÉRALE VICOMTESSE DE VIBRAYE*'

Hydrangea macrophylla

A large group of deciduous shrubs, which can form an ornamental hedge up to 6ft (2m) high and of broader spread. The glossy leaves are oval, pointed, and coarsely toothed and up to 8in (20cm) long. The flowers are formed into rounded heads of large flowers (Hortensias or mopheads), or flattish heads of many tiny flowers surrounded by a few large flowers (Lacecaps). There are many cultivars to choose from, with flowers in white, blue, or pink. Flower color is influenced by both cultivar and soil acidity. On acid soil blue flowering is encouraged, ranging through shades of pink in more alkaline soils. On neutral soils blue color can be maintained with regular applications of aluminum sulfate to the soil. Hydrangeas are easily grown in moisture-retentive soil. Prune and deadhead in late autumn to reduce the number of shoots. ◫–◪◊ Z6–9
'Mariesii Perfecta' *p.28*

I

Ilex aquifolium
(English holly)
Although fairly slow growing, this evergreen holly (*p.32*) makes a very good hedge, giving bold decorative form and dense, thorny protection. The hard, glossy, dark green leaves are 2–4in (5–10cm) long with wavy, spine-bearing margins. Male and female flowers are borne on different plants, and a mix gives rise to the scarlet or orange berries, which can persist into winter, subject to bird feeding. There are numerous cultivars, many of which have variegated leaves, some with smooth margins, others densely prickly, and some with yellow berries. Also successful for hedging are the other evergreen hollies
I. × aquipernyi, I. cornuta, I. × meserveae, I. crenata, and *I. × altaclerensis,* all of which also have many cultivars. Trim regularly in summer. ◫–◪◊ Z6–9
I. × meserveae 'Blue Princess' *p.30*

ILEX AQUIFOLIUM

J

Juniperus chinensis
A hardy conifer with strongly scented, tough, dark green foliage. It can be successfully grown as a contained hedge, as can *J. virginiana.* There are many cultivars of varying habit and color. Trim in summer; do not cut into older wood; it will not resprout. ◫–◪◊ Z3–9

K

Kerria japonica
A deciduous shrub that suckers to form a thicket and is suitable for an informal flowering hedge. The double-flowered form 'Pleniflora' is an upright plant growing to 6ft (2m); single-flowered plants are lower and more spreading in shape. Prune in late spring after flowering, either removing flowered shoots to ground level or reducing them to various lengths. Spreading growths will need to be dug out. ◫–◪◊ Z4–9

KERRIA JAPONICA

L

Laurus nobilis
(Bay laurel)
An evergreen plant with dark green, aromatic foliage, the leaves 4in (10cm) long. Plants are susceptible to frost, so bay is best planted as an internal hedge. The cultivar 'Aurea' has gold leaves and is an interesting variation, but usually better as a specimen plant. Laurel is long lived under fertile, moist soil conditions and is a proven choice for topiary work. In hedge plantings or as topiary it should be trained to formal shape by summer clipping.
◨–▨◊ Z8–10

Lavandula angustifolia
(Lavender)
A compact plant (p.22) up to 3ft (1m) high with linear, aromatic, gray-green leaves, 2in (5cm) long. Attractive for its dense spikes of fragrant, blue flowers, which appear in midsummer and keep their form as they dry on the plant. Does well in full sun on a wide range of sites and soils,

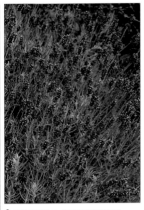

LAVANDULA ANGUSTIFOLIA 'HIDCOTE'

and is excellent for a low hedge or edging. Trim close below faded flowering spikes in early spring. There are a number of cultivars, and the compact 'Hidcote' with dark purple flowers and 'Loddon Pink' are worth seeking. Plants eventually become woody and straggly, so it is best to replant hedges after about ten years.
▨◊ Z5–8

Leycesteria formosa
(Himalayan honeysuckle, pheasant bush)
A thicket-forming, deciduous shrub growing up to 6ft (2m) and suitable as an informal hedge plant where year-round cover is not essential. It tolerates a wide range of soil conditions and exposure. The young stems are attractive, bamboolike, and dark green, and bear long, pendent spikes of white flowers surrounded by wine-red bracts. Maroon to purple-black fruits follow. For the best stem effect, cut the plant to 2–4in (5–10cm) above ground level in spring.
◨–▨◊ Z9–10

Ligustrum ovalifolium
(California privet, Z6–8)
A widely grown evergreen, which may be deciduous in coastal and cooler areas, with rich green leaves 2½in (6cm) long. The cultivar 'Aureum' (golden privet) has broad leaves with bright yellow margins. Several privets are excellent for formal hedges and topiary shaping, including L. vulgare (common privet, Z5–8) and its variegated cultivars, L. obtusifolium, (Z3–7), with leaves that turn purple in autumn, and L. sinense, (Z7–9) a longer-leaved species, its cultivar 'Variegatum' has pale green leaves with white margins.

These are all fast-growing, tough plants, good in any well-drained soil, in sun or partial shade; the variegated forms are best grown in full sun. Repeated clipping in summer produces the best specimen hedges and topiary. Can be cut hard in spring to restore shape and keep within bounds, but variegated forms often revert. Clipping removes the unpleasantly scented flowers.
◨–▨◊ Zones vary

LAURUS NOBILIS

LEYCESTERIA FORMOSA

Lonicera nitida 'Baggesen's Gold'

Lonicera nitida
(Boxleaf honeysuckle **Z6–9**)
A dense evergreen with tough shoots bearing small, glossy green leaves, lighter on the underside and ½in (1cm) long. Very fast growing, it should be trimmed hard several times each summer to avoid a tendency to straggle. This tolerance of clipping makes it a good candidate for simple topiary forms. If hedges become unkempt or bare at the base they can usually be rejuvenated by cutting down to within 6in (15cm) of ground level. All such severe cutting should be carried out progressively over more than one season. 'Baggesen's Gold' is a yellow-leaved cultivar. *Lonicera tatarica* (**Z3–9**) is another bushy species sometimes grown as an informal hedge, and the shrubby, deciduous *L. fragrantissima* (**Z5–8**) can be used as a flowering hedge, producing tubular, fragrant, creamy white flowers in winter and early spring. Climbing honeysuckles can also be grown on a structure to form a "fedge" (*p.7*). Cut out old or weak stems of *L. fragrantissima* and *L. tatarica* in summer after flowering, and shorten one in three of the other stems.
◧–◙◊ **Zones vary**

M

Maclura pomifera
(Osage orange)
A dense, spiny shrub with deep orange bark, suitable as a protective hedge. Leaves are 4in (10cm) long and green, turning yellow in autumn. Where male and female plants are grown together, inedible, orange-sized fruits will be produced. Tolerates trimming to shape in spring.
◧◊ **Z5–9**

Mahonia aquifolium
(Oregon grapeholly)
The mahonias are resilient, evergreen shrubs with striking leaves made up of spiky leaflets. *Mahonia aquifolium* is low growing, to 3ft (1m), with tough leaves up to 12in (30cm) long. Bears densely

Maclura pomifera

Myrtus communis

clustered yellow flowers in spring, which are followed by blue-black berries. Perhaps the toughest mahonia, good even in dry shade.
   M. japonica and its Bealei Group cultivars, together with cultivars of *M. × media*, can make taller, spiny hedges with arching sprays of fragrant, yellow flowers borne from autumn to late winter. Minimal pruning is needed beyond occasional removal of some older stems.
◙–◙◊ **Z6–9**

Myrtus communis
(Common myrtle)
An upright, bushy evergreen to 10ft (3m), with glossy, aromatic leaves to 2in (5cm) long. In late summer myrtle bears attractive, small, white flowers, each with a prominent bunch of whiskery stamens; these are followed by purple-black berries. Good for exposed seaside gardens. Requires minimal pruning in spring.
Z8–9

NERIUM OLEANDER
'PETITE SALMON'

OLEARIA MACRODONTA

OSMANTHUS DELAVAYI

N

Nerium oleander
(Oleander)
An upright evergreen to 8ft
(2.5m) with narrow, leathery
leaves and clusters of tubular,
pink flowers from summer to
autumn. Occasionally seen to
good effect as a hedge in areas
with low risk of frost. Tender
plants such as this can form
temporary hedges if container-
grown specimens are brought
out from winter protection to
form a short hedge run. The
cultivar 'Petite Red' shows
fair hardiness. Little pruning
is required; cut shoot tips in
late summer or autumn after
flowering. Plants are toxic if
eaten; foliage may irritate skin.
(min. 36°F/2°C)

O

Olearia macrodonta
(Arorangi, Daisy bush, New
Zealand holly)
A vigorous, upright plant with
glossy, dark green, hollylike
leaves, silver felted on the
underside, 4in (10cm) long.
Bears white, fragrant daisy
flowers in clusters during the
summer. Excellent for coastal
gardens. Best trimmed lightly
after flowering to maintain an
orderly shape.
Several other daisy bushes
are also good hedging shrubs:
O. solandri and *O. virgata*
have narrow leaves and
smaller flowers, *O.* × *haastii* is
the hardiest and also tolerates
pollution, while *O. traversii*
is one of the fastest-growing
windbreaks for coastal areas.
Z9–10

Osmanthus delavayi
The tough, glossy, dark green
leaves, to 1in (2.5cm) long,
make this evergreen a very
handsome hedge when it is
trimmed. The clusters of
jasminelike, tubular, white
flowers, borne in late spring,
are highly fragrant. An
adaptable plant, which should
be lightly trimmed in summer.
It is slow growing, eventually
reaching 6ft (2m).
Also slow growing is the
species *O. heterophyllus*, a
mildly spiny alternative of
which there are a number of
interesting variants including
the excellent 'Goshiki' which
has leaves that are mottled
yellow and bronze when
young, and 'Gulftide', a dense
plant with conspicuous spines
to the leaves.
–Z7–9

P

Perovskia atriplicifolia
An upright plant growing to
4ft (1.2m) tall, with gray
shoots and aromatic leaves to
2in (5cm) long. Bears airy,
branching spikes of small,
tubular, violet-blue flowers in
tall spikes from late summer
to early autumn. *Perovskia*
'Blue Spire' is noted for its
profuse flowering. Tolerates
alkaline soil and dry or
coastal conditions. An
interesting free-growing
hedge, and useful interplanted
with trimmed lavender
(*Lavandula*, *p.67*) as an
edging. For the best foliage,
prune hard in spring, taking
the stems back to the base.
Z6–9

Philadelphus coronarius
(Mock orange)
An upright, deciduous shrub suitable as an informal hedge subject, growing up to 10ft (3m) tall, with leaves 4in (10cm) long. The greatest attraction is the small bunches of intensely fragrant, white, saucer-shaped flowers 1in (2.5cm) across, borne in early summer. Its cultivars include 'Aureus', which bears golden yellow to lime green leaves on a more compact plant, and 'Variegatus', which has leaves with broad white margins. Easily grown on well-drained soil in full or partial sun.

Annual pruning is necessary to maintain flowering shoots; cut out around one in four flowered shoots in late summer, after flowering. Cultivars such as 'Aureus' are best pruned in late spring, just before flowering, to enhance the foliage effect. There are also many excellent hybrid cultivars worth considering, including 'Buckley's Quill' to 6ft (2m) high, 'Belle Etoile', and 'Manteau d'Hermine'.
◧–◧◊ Z5–8

Photinia × *fraseri*
Vigorous, versatile evergreen to 15ft (5m), with leaves that are bright red when young, maturing to dark green. There are several good cultivars including the vivid 'Red Robin' and the hardy 'Robusta'. *Photinia serratifolia* with copper colored young leaves is also used. Prune lightly to shape in spring, or trim as a formal hedge in spring and summer.
◧–◧◊ Z8–9

Picea abies
(Norway spruce)
An evergreen conifer, widely cultivated on a range of moisture-retentive soils. The conical frame bears level or drooping branches with pendulous branchlets; the dark green, needle-like leaves are 1in (2.5cm) long. Spruce trees are often successfully grown as screen hedges, planted close together. They are slow to develop but make an elegant feature for suitable parts of a large garden, especially where plans can be laid for a boundary to obscure traffic and lessen noise. The least possible pruning should be done.
◧–◧◊ Z3–8

Pittosporum tenuifolium
A fast-establishing, large, bushy shrub with tough, glossy, green leaves 1–2½in (2.5–6cm) long, usually with wavy edges. Especially good in coastal gardens; there are many interesting cultivars. *Pittosporum crassifolium* has larger, thicker leaves. Trim to shape in spring and autumn.
◧–◧◊ Z9–10

Podocarpus macrophyllus
(Kumasaki)
A generally robust, usually shrubby conifer. Bears lance-shaped, leathery leaves 2½–4in (6–10cm) long, light green when young, darkening as they mature. Prefers a humid environment, sheltered from cold or dry winds. Together with *P. nivalis* it can be trimmed to shape in spring as an attractive hedge, doing well on a wide range of soils but not in exposed sites.
◧◊ Z7–10

PHILADELPHUS
'BUCKLEY'S QUILL'

PHOTINIA × FRASERI
'RED ROBIN'

PITTOSPORUM TENUIFOLIUM

PONICIRUS TRIFOLIATA

Poncirus trifoliata
(Hardy orange)
A formidable, thorny shrub with thick, green shoots armed with sharp spines. The leaves, made up of 3 leaflets, each 1–2½in (2½–6cm) long, are dark green, turning yellow in autumn. Fragrant, cup-shaped, white flowers are produced in spring, with a second flush in autumn. Orangelike but inedible fruits 1½in (4cm) in diameter are produced. Needs well-drained soil and does best in full sun. Cut young plants hard to help them establish, and trim hedges twice in summer.
⌑◊ Z5–9

Potentilla fruticosa
A compact shrub to 3ft (1m) high, which can be used to form a low, spreading hedge. The compound leaves are 1½in (4cm) in length and made up of six or so narrow leaflets. Bears saucer-shaped, yellow flowers continuously from spring to autumn. There are many cultivars with different flower colors from white through shades of

yellow, pink, and orange to bright red. Trim over lightly after flowering, removing straggly growth and cutting out a small proportion of the oldest wood.
⌑◊ Z3–7
'Vilmoriniana' p.26

Prunus laurocerasus
(Cherry laurel)
A large, dense, evergreen shrub with glossy leaves up to 6in (15cm) long, which are dark green above and pale green below. Produces showy clustered, short spikes of white flowers in spring, followed by red, cherrylike fruits that ripen to black. There are many selections, including the bushy 'Rotundifolia' which is vigorous, upright, and a good hedge subject, and 'Otto Luyken', which has narrow, dark leaves and reliably produces flowers in late spring and autumn where grown informally or semi-formally. *Prunus lusitanica*, the Portugal laurel, is another similar evergreen also suitable for hedging. Trim to shape

POTENTILLA FRUTICOSA 'SUNSET'

PRUNUS LAUROCERASUS 'ZABELIANA'

with pruners in the spring. All parts of these may cause severe discomfort if eaten.
⌑–⌑◊ Z6–9

Prunus spinosa
(Blackthorn, Sloe)
A dense, thorny shrub with deep green leaves, 2in (5cm) long. Small, white flowers are borne in spring before the leaves appear and are followed by black fruits with a blue bloom in autumn, which remain on the bush into winter; these are edible, but bitter. Blackthorn makes a good protective barrier and tolerates hard trimming at any time. The cultivar 'Purpurea' has red leaves turning to purple and bears pink flowers. Also used for hedging is *P. cerasifera*, the myrobalan, which is similarly deciduous and flowers on bare wood in spring, but is not thorny: the fruits are edible and red or yellow. The cultivar 'Nigra' (p.33) with pink flowers and leaves that are red when young, maturing to dark purple, is often grown.
⌑◊ Z5–9

Pseudosasa japonica
(Bamboo)

A hardy bamboo, growing up to 15ft (5m) tall, so suitable only for special purposes, such as an outer windbreak hedge or screen. *Fargesia nitida* (fountain bamboo) is an elegant, dense, clump-forming bamboo, slow growing and marked by purple branchlets on the upper part of the canes, bearing cascades of narrow, dark green leaves. There are several cultivars of this fine bamboo. *Phyllostachys* species are also suitable for hedge screens, and there are forms with attractive leaves and stem coloring: *P. aurea* (fishpole bamboo) is strongly erect with dense foliage and stems maturing from bright green to yellow, and *P. nigra* (black bamboo) is notable for its black stems. Bamboos will grow in any well-drained soil, and can give useful shelter. They are slow to establish but do become invasive with time, requiring annual thinning and width reduction.
▣ –▨◊ Z7–10

PYRACANTHA 'GOLDEN CHARMER'

Pyracantha coccinea
(Scarlet firethorn)

A thick, bushy, very spiny, evergreen shrub (*p.26, p.30*) to 12ft (4m), with dark green leaves. Useful as a barrier hedge because of its spiny habit and also attractive for the profuse red berries borne in autumn, following creamy white flowers in early summer. Pyracanthas are easy to grow in most soils in sun or shade. Best thinned at least twice annually as a formal hedge, in spring and summer. The plants are susceptible to fireblight disease.
▣ –▨◊ Z6–9

Q

Quercus ilex
(Holly oak, Holm oak Z7–9)

Naturally a very large tree. Slow growing, with dark green, glossy, leathery leaves 3in (8cm) long, and a suitable subject for a contained hedge. The natural shedding of the oldest leaves in spring can be a nuisance. Trim to formal

QUERCUS ILEX

shape in spring. *Quercus robur* (English oak Z5–8) and *Q. rubra* (Northern red oak Z5–9) are valuable additions to hedges on garden borders.
▣◊ Zones vary

R

Rhamnus frangula
(Alder buckthorn Z3–8)

A bushy, variably spiny, deciduous shrub with thick, glossy, dark green leaves 3in (7cm) long, which turn red in autumn. Small, yellow-green flowers are borne in clusters along the shoots in late spring and early summer, followed by red berries ripening to black. It makes a useful formal hedge on any moist soil and in shade or sun, as does the common buckthorn, *Rhamnus cathartica* Z3–8, also deciduous and widely grown as a spiny hedge, with prolific shiny berries ripening from red to black in autumn. *R. alaternus* (Italian buckthorn Z7–9) is an evergreen shrub that will stand both coastal and

PSEUDOSASA JAPONICA

industrial air exposure well. The 'Argenteovariegata' cultivar has white margins to the green leaves. All parts of these plants are poisonous if eaten. Trim to hedge shape in spring.

◨–◙◊ **Zones vary**

Rhaphiolepis umbellata

A dense, slow-growing, generally hardy evergreen, naturally up to 5ft (1.5m) tall, with tough, dark green, toothed leaves 3½in (9cm) long. Bears clusters of white flowers, sometimes tinted with pink, in early summer, followed by bronze-black fruits. Trim to shape after flowering.

◨◊ **Z8–10**

Rhododendron

Many rhododendrons make spectacular hedges on moist, well-drained, humus-rich soil. Evergreen species are most suitable. *Rhododendron ponticum* **Z6–9**, a dominant species, is evergreen with glossy, dark green leaves 2½–7in (6–18cm) long and bears trusses of broad, trumpet-shaped, mauve to lilac flowers in late spring, providing an attractive display as a vigorous, informal hedge in larger gardens. If rhododendrons appeal and the soil conditions are suitable, it is best to learn which ones grow in local gardens or nurseries or seek expert advice; there is an immense range of azaleas and rhododendrons available, and the best flowering cultivars are a considerable investment. Allow to grow informally, with minimal pruning.

◙ ᵖᴴ ◊ **Zones vary**

Ribes sanguineum

(Flowering currant **Z6–8**) An upright, deciduous shrub, 6ft (2m) tall with dark green, hairy leaves 2–4in (5–10cm) long. It makes an attractive informal hedge in the garden, with a fine display of pendent flower clusters. Flowering currants are robust and will establish well on most soils. The majority do best in a location with full sun.

Cultivars worth considering include the compact 'King Edward VII', which bears dark red flowers, and 'Pulborough Scarlet', which has dark red flowers with white centers. The yellow-leaved cultivar 'Brocklebankii' is slow growing, and for the best leaf effect it should be grown out of full sun.

Ribes alpinum **Z2–6** is a choice where a hedge of no more than 36in (90cm) height is appropriate, and tolerates shade; male and female plants must be grown together for flower production. The female cultivar 'Aureum' has bright yellow leaves.

◨–▥◊ **Zones vary**

ROSA RUGOSA

ROSMARINUS OFFICINALIS

Rosa

(Rose) Roses provide a popular garden feature suitable for a large range of situations. They are grown in beds, borders, and some as hedges. Mostly **Z5–9**; many require winter cover. *Rosa rugosa* **Z2–9** (Hedgehog rose, Sea tomato), a vigorous, dense species with very prickly stems, dark green leaves, and fragrant flowers followed by large red-orange hips, is a popular choice for hedging.

◨◊ **Zones vary**

Rosmarinus officinalis

(Rosemary) Attains a hedge height of up to 5ft (1.5m). The upright shoots bear linear, leathery, aromatic green leaves and blue flowers along the shoot length in spring and autumn. Grow in a sunny spot in moderately fertile soil. Informal hedges require minimal pruning only. With careful management, rosemary can be maintained as a formal hedge clipped twice during the summer.

◨◊ **Z8–10**

S

Salix
(Willow)

The willows are a diverse and extensive group of deciduous plants, ranging from large trees to procumbent shrubs. They include some types that can be considered for use in informal or semiformal hedges and screens.

Salix alba (white willow Z4–9) makes a good external shelter hedge on windy, open sites. There are a number of selections, including *S. alba* subsp. *vitellina*, which produces yellow to orange winter shoots, and its cultivar 'Britzensis' with orange to red winter shoots. All are fast growing and will exceed 20ft (7m) in height.

S. lanata (woolly willow Z3–5) makes a low hedge to about 3ft (1m) and is notable for its golden yellow male catkins or gray-yellow female catkins in spring. All willows bear catkins, usually with the male and female flowers on different plants.

SALIX ALBA SUBSP. VITELLINA 'BRITZENSIS'

SAMBUCUS NIGRA 'GUINCHO PURPLE'

The requirements of willows are not exacting, except that the soil must be adequately moist all year; willows will succeed on wet sites where other plants fail. Their roots seek out moisture over some distance, and none should be planted close to building foundations or drains: willow roots can invade, weaken, penetrate, and choke.

Willow hedges are best coppiced – cut back to the base annually to maintain new wood growth for color and catkins. Where year-round wind protection or screening is wanted they can be allowed to grow unchecked for several seasons or partly cut each year. All willows are easily propagated from hardwood cuttings.
◫◊ **Zones vary**

Sambucus nigra
(Black elder, Elderberry)

Upright, potentially very tall, deciduous plant with pinnate leaves up to 10in (25cm) long. Bears flattened heads of musk-scented, white flowers in early summer, followed by clusters of glossy, black fruit. 'Guincho Purple' has dark green leaves, which become very dark and then red in autumn; they color best in full sun, but retain the color better in light shade. Grow in moderately fertile, humus-rich soil. A good border hedge choice. Prune regularly in winter, cutting old stems to ground level and shortening most of the rest.
◫ – ◪◊ **Z6–8**

Santolina chamaecyparissus
(Lavender cotton)

A low, evergreen hedging subject up to 24in (60cm) tall, with slender, aromatic, gray leaves. Produces small, buttonlike, bright yellow daisy flowers in mid- to late summer. Some cultivars with paler leaves or flowers are available, any of which are very suitable as edging. Prefers poor to moderately fertile soil. Trim after flowering to remove straggly shoots, and at 3–4 year intervals cut back hard in the spring to rejuvenate.
◫◊ **Z6–9**

SANTOLINA CHAMAECYPARISSUS 'LEMON QUEEN'

SARCOCCOA HOOKERIANA
VAR. *DIGYNA* 'PURPLE STEM'

Sarcococca hookeriana
(Christmas box, Sweet box)
An adaptable evergreen up to
5ft (1.5m) high with dark,
glossy leaves 3½in (9cm) long.
Valuable for its fragrant,
white flowers, borne in
clusters during winter months
and followed by spherical,
black fruits. Best in deep or
partial shade; in sun, be sure
that the soil remains moist.
Tolerates pollution but needs
shelter from cold and drying
winds. Interesting as an
informal hedging plant; the
little pruning necessary should
be done in spring.
◨-◼◊Z6–9

Sorbus intermedia
(Swedish whitebeam Z6–8)
A deciduous, compact tree
with toothed, dark green
leaves, gray on the underside,
5in (12cm) long. A line of
whitebeams planted 3ft (1m)
apart can form a sturdy
windbreak, narrow hedge, or
screen. It succeeds on a wide
range of soils and in coastal
and urban situations. Dense,
flattened clusters of white
flowers add interest in the

spring, and red berries are
produced in the autumn. Can
be clipped in summer, at the
expense of the berries. *Sorbus
aria* (Whitebeam) can be
grown similarly; the cultivar
'Lutescens' is a good choice.
S. americana (Mountain ash
Z3–8) is good for exposed
boundary hedges. All are
susceptible to fireblight.
◨-◼◊Zones vary

Spiraea japonica
A sturdy, upright, deciduous
plant to 6ft (2m). The dark
green, toothed leaves are gray
below and 5in (12cm) long.
Prominent, flattened heads of
clustered, small, pink flowers
are borne in late summer. The
leaves of 'Anthony Waterer'
(*p.29*) are bronze when young
and often margined with
white. *Spiraea* 'Arguta' and
S. × vanhouttei are among
many other spireas suitable as
informal hedging. Grows in
most soils in full sun. After
flowering prune the flowered
shoots back to a strong bud
and cut a number of older
shoots to ground level.
◨◊Z4–8

SYMPHORICARPOS ALBUS
VAR. *LAEVIGATUS*

SYRINGA × CHINENSIS 'ALBA'

Symphoricarpos albus
(Snowberry)
A dense, upright, robust
evergreen to 6ft (2m) with
dark green leaves, producing
bell-shaped, pink flowers
during the summer, followed
by spherical, pure white fruits.
Effective on a wide range of
sites, producing a hedge up to
6ft (2m) high. Can be invasive
so best suited to borders,
where it could be included
in a mixed hedge. Prune
selectively to the base in early
spring to contain spread and
to keep rejuvenated.
◨-◼◊Z3–7

Syringa × chinensis
(Lilac)
Bushy, deciduous shrub to
12ft (4m) high, with fragrant
flowers in the spring. Bears
oval leaves 3in (8cm) long.
There are many species of
lilac and numerous cultivars
also worthy of consideration
for informal hedging. They
require minimal pruning, after
flowering, but are amenable
to occasional hard pruning to
rejuvenate plants.
◨◊Z5–8

T

Tamarix ramosissima
(Tamarisk Z3–8)
A versatile, deciduous shrub up to 15ft (5m) high with brown shoots bearing very small, pointed, feathery leaves ⅛in (4mm) long. It produces pink flowers in dense, spike-like heads in summer and autumn. Suitable for coastal hedging, growing best in well-drained soil, but requiring moister soil and shelter from cold and drying winds inland. Becomes straggly if not hard pruned regularly to shape in early spring. *Tamarix tetrandra*, Z5–9, is a similar but shorter and less hardy shrub that flowers earlier, in mid- to late spring.
🔳◊–◊ **Zones vary**

Taxus baccata
(Yew Z7–8)
A well-proven, coniferous hedge plant (*p.8, p.20*) with small, linear, dark green leaves ¾–1¼in (2–3cm) long borne on green shoots. Male plants produce yellow cones in

TAMARIX RAMOSISSIMA

TAXUS BACCATA

spring, which give rise to the small, red, seed-bearing fruits on female plants. All parts of the plant are toxic except for the red, fleshy covering of the seeds. Will grow in sun or shade in any fertile, well-drained soil. An excellent choice for topiary. *Taxus cuspidata*, the Japanese yew, and *T.* × *media* also make suitable hedges, Z5–7. Yews are amenable to hard trimming in late summer. *Cephalotaxus harringtonii*, Z6–9, is a yewlike conifer with pale brown fruits, which is also suitable for hedging.
🔳–🔳◊ **Zones vary**

Teucrium lucidrys
syn. *T. chamaedrys*
(Wall germander)
A shrubby evergreen growing up to 20in (50cm) tall and suitable as a very low hedge. The dark green, aromatic leaves are 1½in (4cm) long and have toothed edges. If it is not trimmed in spring, red, pink, purple, or white flowers are produced in summer. Prune in spring or trim to a formal shape in summer.
🔳◊ **Z5–9**

Thuja plicata
(Western red cedar Z6–8)
A vigorous, coniferous species, naturally growing to be a tree but amenable to trimming into a formal hedge. The leaves are dark green and aromatic, borne in graceful, hanging sprays. Grow in sun or shade in any deep, well-drained soil and provide shelter from winds, especially when young. Trimming should be done several times throughout the summer for best results. *Thuja occidentalis*, White cedar Z2–7, is robust and suitable for hedging.
🔳◊ **Zones vary**

Tsuga heterophylla
(Western hemlock)
A fast-growing, pinelike conifer with pendent tips to the branches, bearing glossy, dark green, narrow leaves ¼–¾in (0.5–2cm) long. Like other hemlocks, it is tolerant of shade, but it will not grow well in alkaline soils. Suitable for formal trimming during the summer months.
🔳–🔳 ᵖᴴ **Z6–8**

THUJA PLICATA

U

Ulmus
(Elm)

Hardy, deciduous trees, common in thickets and garden hedges before Dutch elm disease destroyed most North American and European elms. *Ulmus minor* (European field elm) and its cultivars 'Cornubiensis' (Cornish elm) and 'Sarniensis' (Jersey elm) make good windbreaks that stand well in coastal areas. Saplings of these and *U. procera* (English elm) often reestablish and grow to 10ft (3m) or so before again succumbing to infection. *U. pumila* has lance-shaped, toothed, dark green leaves and tiny red flowers; it may have partial resistance to Dutch elm disease, as does its cultivar 'Sapporo Autumn Gold'. Also used is *U. parvifolia,* which is sometimes semi-evergreen with a shrubby form when young; it has some resistance to Dutch elm disease.
◨–◩◊ Z5–8

ULMUS PUMILA

VIBURNUM TINUS

V

Viburnum tinus
(Laurustinus Z8–10)

Evergreen or deciduous shrubs with ornamental leaves, often fragrant flowers, and interesting fruits. They can be used for formal or informal hedging. *Viburnum tinus* is an evergreen up to 10ft (3m) high with dark green leaves to 4in (10cm) long and flattened heads of small, white flowers for an extended period in winter and spring, followed by small, dark blue fruits. 'Gwenllian' has pink buds and pink-flushed flowers. Also worth trying is 'Eve Price'. Grow as an informal hedge or trim closely in early summer after flowering.

Deciduous types make good informal hedges where winter cover is not essential. *V. opulus* (Guelder rose Z4–8) grows to 15ft (5m), with maplelike, dark green leaves that turn red in autumn. Flat heads of white flowers in late spring and early summer are followed by red, fleshy fruits; the cultivar

'Xanthocarpum' has yellow fruits. *V.* × *carlcephalum,* **Z6–8**, reaches 10ft (3m), the dark green leaves turning red in autumn. Round clusters of fragrant, white flowers open from pink buds in the spring. *V. carlesii* is shorter, to 6ft (2m) high, with smaller leaves and less dense flowerheads, followed by red fruits that ripen black. Minimal trimming is needed and should be done in summer.
◨–◩◊ Zones vary

W

Weigela florida

Deciduous, spreading shrub up to 8ft (2.5m) high with dark green leaves borne on arching shoots, suitable for an informal hedge. The dark pink, funnel-shaped flowers open in late spring to early summer. The cultivar 'Foliis Purpureis', to 3ft (1m) high, has bronze leaves. Reduce flowered stems in number and length in midsummer after flowering.
◨–◩◊ Z5–8

WEIGELA FLORIDA 'FOLIIS PURPUREIS'

INDEX

Page numbers in **bold italics** refer to illustrated information

ACKNOWLEDGMENTS

Picture Research Anna Grapes
Picture Librarian Romaine Werblow
Special photography Peter Anderson,
Trish Gant, Gary Ombler
Illustrations Karen Gavin

Index Hilary Bird

Dorling Kindersley would like to thank:
All staff at the RHS, in particular Susanne
Mitchell, Karen Wilson, and Barbara Haynes
at Vincent Square, and Dean Peckett and Jim
England at Wisley; Joanna Chisholm and
Candida Frith-Macdonald for editorial
assistance; Ann Thompson for design
assistance.

American Horticultural Society
Visit the **AHS** at www.ahs.org or call them at
1-800-777-7631 ext. 119. Membership

benefits include *The American Gardener*
magazine, free admission to flower shows,
the free seed exchange, book services, and the
Gardener's Information Service.

Photography
The publisher would also like to thank the
following for their kind permission to
reproduce their photographs:
(key: t=top, c=center, b=below, l=left, r=right)

Echo Hedgecutter photograph courtesy of
Countax Ltd: 46t
John Glover: 11tl, 21tl, 21cr, 23t, 33tl
M. R. Pollock: 7bl, 8b, 11cr, 14br, 25, 31,
32br, 46tl, 48br
Royal Horticultural Society, Wisley: 52cr,
52clb, 52bc, 52br, 52bl.
Steven Wooster: 2, garden by Tom Stuart-
Smith; jacket flap, garden by Anne Maynard
and Piet Oudolf.